LIBERALISM, CHILDHOOD AND JUSTICE

Ethical Issues in Upbringing

Timothy Fowler

BRISTOL
UNIVERSITY
PRESS

This paperback editon first published in Great Britain in 2021 by

Bristol University Press
University of Bristol
1-9 Old Park Hill
Bristol
BS2 8BB
UK
t: +44 (0)117 954 5940
e: bup-info@bristol.ac.uk

Details of international sales and distribution partners are available at
bristoluniversitypress.co.uk

British Library Cataloguing in Publication Data
A catalogue record for this book is available from the British Library

ISBN 978-1-5292-0164-2 paperback
ISBN 978-1-5292-0163-5 hardcover
ISBN 978-1-5292-0166-6 ePub
ISBN 978-1-5292-0165-9 ePdf

Cover design by Blu Inc

Front cover image: Samuel Zeller, Unsplash

Bristol University Press and Policy Press use environmentally
responsible print partners.

Printed in Great Britain by CPI Group (UK) Ltd, Croydon,
CR0 4YY

To my parents, from whom I received an upbringing that has enabled me to flourish

Contents

Acknowledgements

I'd like to thank all the people who've supported me through the process of writing this book. Intellectually I owe a great deal to the political theory communities of Bristol, Warwick, York and Pompeu Fabra, especially to Matthew Clayton, Esther Dermott, Anca Gheaus, Andrew Williams, Chris Bertram, Liam Shields, Serena Olsaretti, Anne Stevens and Christina Easton. The book would not exist without the support I've had from Charlotte Miller, who in this, as in so much, has been a source of great strength and fortitude. Most of all I'd like to thank my parents, to whom I dedicate this book.

Introduction

This book considers children's place in liberal theory and develops a novel account of what justice requires with respect to children and how relations between adults should be arranged to best achieve this. While the last decade has seen a flourishing debate on children's rights and entitlements, these issues remain relatively peripheral to theoretical debates. The case of children is largely seen as an addendum to be worked out once the central questions of justice between adults have been decided upon. Witness the relatively brief considerations of childhood in the works of the great liberal thinkers of the last century such as John Rawls, Joseph Raz and Ronald Dworkin. Their methods were to begin with the questions of justice that arise between adults, come to some set of principles that solves these matters, then show how those same principles can be *applied* to children. In contrast, I propose that children must be much more central to political thinking, and that taking their claims seriously means rethinking central elements in leading theories of justice and challenging core elements of received liberal thinking.

Childhood matters for many reasons, but centrally because the nature of childhood undermines the persistent myth that people are best conceived only as independent actors whose outcomes are down to their own choices. Children require the constant care and attention of adults to ensure their very survival. The ways that older children think and act is greatly influenced by the social context in which they grew up. A child's access to social and economic advantages early in life is a central determinant of their later level of economic and social advantage. In these ways, and many others, the shape and success of a person's life is determined by the way that other, older, people live theirs. Children are thus a powerful example of the interdependence between people and the extent to which any one person's projects and life choices are intertwined with the choices of others. Thinking through the case of childhood thus delivers a theory of justice better suited to the reality of interdependent social creatures than to the idealized autonomous subject that underlies much liberal thought.

Children's radical dependence on others, and the degree to which their very personality is shaped by social influences, matters in many respects, but I will centrally explore the importance of childhood for understanding the relationship between matters of *ethics* – what makes for a flourishing life – and matters of *justice* – what principles should shape our interactions with one another. In a classic discussion on the foundations of liberal theory, Ronald Dworkin (1990: 16–22) suggests two ways of understanding the liberal project: the discontinuous and the continuous. The discontinuous view sees justice as being fundamentally separate from ethics such that a person can accept liberalism regardless of their own private ethical beliefs. The continuous view sees politics as inseparable from ethics, such that the justification for liberal institutions flows from the belief that they will promote the flourishing of citizens. This basic divide suggests two very different pictures about what a liberal society should look like. Defenders of liberal neutrality believe that principles of justice must take no position on what constitutes a good human life. They see liberalism as a system for ensuring cooperation between people who are profoundly divided on matters of ethics, culture and religion. In contrast, so-called liberal perfectionists believe that liberalism must be animated by a view about the elements that ensure human flourishing; for them, autonomous agency is central to such flourishing.

This philosophical divide has many consequences in practice, some of the most important of which directly affect children. Liberal neutralists believe it is wrong for the state, or wider society, to try and use schools or other institutions to promote good living. Since society cannot permissibly favour any particular ethical or religious views, it cannot coherently require that children's upbringing is guided by any such ideals. Promoting autonomy requires a more interventionist approach; for perfectionists the emphasis is on developing children's critical reflection and ensuring that all children have access to a wide variety of different options as they grow up.

While I embrace the perfectionist approach, I will show that both varieties of liberalism have failed to offer an adequate account of children's justice, though the problems are more severe for the neutralist picture. The problem with liberal neutrality is that, when thinking about adults, the central question of justice is how to respond to or respect a person's already existing belief system. In contrast, children's interest is in the formation of beliefs and values and whether or not the way of life they become socialized into is conducive to them living a good life now or as an adult. Children thus have a powerful interest in having an early environment which enables them to flourish, so knowing what such an environment consists of requires taking a stand on matters of ethics.

While liberal perfectionists are right to think that justice for children is centrally about enabling human flourishing, they have overemphasized the importance of self-direction. While it is vitally important to develop children's skills of critical reasoning and debate, it is deeply mistaken to see the autonomous person as somehow immune from the pervasive influence of his or her parents and wider society. As such, an excessive focus on autonomy valorizes independence without recognizing the importance of humans' mutual dependence. Human flourishing, especially children's, requires a background culture that enables personal relationships to flourish. My own theory is thus a perfectionist one; it locates the role of justice as promoting well-being but locates this value in building flourishing interpersonal relationships and accessing the natural world, in addition to familiar liberal goods such as freedom of choice.

Fleshing out this aim requires building an account of well-being and a view about how it is best promoted and sustained. I argue that well-being consists of the achievement of objectively valuable goods and that many of the most important goods in life require engagement both in childhood and adulthood. I also contend that society has a duty to promote children's well-being as far as is possible, consistent with the other demands of justice, but that a special priority of justice should be promoting the well-being of the worst-off children. The distributive implications of this theory are that families and parents must be subsidized by the rest of society to enable them to provide better care to their children and ensure that economic and social divisions between children be significantly reduced. More widely, the book claims that both parents and the state must work to encourage children to have a specified set of values and aspirations. For instance, I argue that morality requires that children be brought up to hold what are often termed 'progressive' opinions on matters of race, gender and class and that they should value the planet and the natural world. This requirement is justified because the well-being of children, often especially the worst-off children, depends upon their social environment and on the beliefs and practices of those around them.

While the debate within liberal theory has mainly been concerned with the activities of the state, I explore the relevance of matters of justice within families and within wider society. In particular, the perfectionist view provides a distinctive view about the role of parents in society. Given the centrality of parenting to some people's lives it is vital that society protects the ability of those who wish to become parents to do so. On the other hand, I argue that parents are duty-bound to promote their children's well-being and lack the wide latitude to shape their child's values that they are granted in contemporary society. While parents are undoubtedly important in children's lives, they are not the only influence on children and, as such, I show why all members of society have reasons to promote the flourishing of children through the culture they collectively create.

In sum, childhood matters for liberal justice because of the extent to which a person's character, choices and values are intertwined with those around him or her, especially while he or she grows up. My central contention is that person can be deeply wronged by the conditions of his or her upbringing in virtue of the values and aspirations he or she comes to hold. Children have an interest in becoming the kind of people who live good lives and this requires that they live in places which foster worthy patterns of life. Becoming such a society requires being considerably more attuned to the ways that our lives are intertwined with one another's through our common practices and subjecting those practices to ethical scrutiny by considering their effects on the youngest and most vulnerable members of society.

Book overview

Part I: Children and Moral Theory

In the first two chapters I discuss the method and subject matter of the book. Primarily, the work offers an ideal normative theory about children's place in liberal society. Such a theory specifies what a perfectly just arrangement would look like. In so doing it offers a standard of assessment that can be used to determine whether different actions or policies bring a society closer to justice. One vital task of a theory is to inform us what changes make a society more just and which would make it less so. This is the *evaluative* function of principles of justice; I discuss why this evaluative function can be performed by an ideal theory even when its recommendations are not feasible and may never become so. I then clarify that while there are many interesting elements of childhood, for the purpose of my theory the most salient are children's *malleability* and their *vulnerability*, which together create a special and radical form of dependence on adults. Children's future aims and projects are conditioned by the choices of those around them. In the rest of the book, I identify which principles of justice are best suited to children, given these features.

Part II: A Distributive Theory for Children

In Chapters 3, 4 and 5, I discuss the core elements of my theory of justice, in particular the metric of children's justice and what principles should guide its distribution. I argue that the dominant resource metric fails to capture important elements of children's interests and that therefore any resource view delivers an impoverished account of children's justice. An adequate account of children's advantage must take account of the ways in which the values and beliefs that children come to hold affect their current and future lives. Through a consideration of what are termed 'the intrinsic goods of childhood', I contend there is a basic case for seeing the start of a person's life as the most important life stage, because gains in childhood are by their nature longer lasting and likely to lead to further advantages later in life. I theorize an account of well-being that highlights the core elements that make for a flourishing childhood.

I then turn to how institutions and social practices should be structured to distribute well-being. I reject the initially attractive principle of distributive equality because this favours levelling down, making the lives of some people worse while making no one's life better. This is problematic since there are many political interventions which can improve the lives of some children without loss to others and I suggest that such interventions are positive steps towards justice. In place of equality I adopt what is known as the priority view, which suggests that the concern of justice should be promoting the welfare of the least-advantaged children.

Part III: Perfectionism and Upbringing

Part III consists of Chapters 6, 7 and 8 and deals with a core principle of liberal theory – ethical neutrality – and the ways this might affect justice for children. According to the neutrality principle, liberal states ought not take sides on contested ethical questions and all policies must be based on things that all reasonable citizens can accept. Across these chapters, I show why this principle of neutrality should be rejected because it has unattractive implications in the case of childhood. Specifically, a theory of justice must be able to measure the impacts of the environment on children's quality of life, but doing so requires defining well-being in a way which violates liberal neutrality. In the language of political theory, I propose a 'perfectionist' account of children's justice.

To defend my perfectionist view, I first reject the leading arguments for liberal neutrality. I then go on to discuss what perfectionism for children entails. In this context, perfectionism refers to the view that the state is empowered to promote people's welfare by taking actions premised on a contested view of ethics. Promoting the welfare of children requires them to come to hold ethical beliefs conducive to their flourishing; they must hold a positive and plausible conception of the good.

I end this part of the book with a discussion of a few examples of what this entails. These are: (i) a personal commitment to gender equality; (ii) knowledge of controversial scientific and historical truths; (iii) an openness with regard to sexual choice; and (iv) a rejection of consumerism. Taken together, these discussions show why justice for children requires them to be raised in an environment conducive to socially liberal beliefs and values, a view that stands in deep tension with theories of liberalism that apply only to politics and to the preferences of many parents.

Part IV: The Rights and Duties of Parents

In Part IV, which consists of four chapters, I discuss the rights and entitlements of parents and their place within my theory. In liberal society, the actions of parents are central to the well-being of children and thus an account of their moral status is a vital part in a theory for children. My twin aims in this part of the book are showing why a robust defence of parental rights is compatible with my theory, but that parents can be held to be under a moral duty to promote good living for children even when they disagree about some issues.

I defend the 'project view' of parenting, according to which parenting should be respected as part of an important project that most people have a right to pursue. I then argue that the best account of parental obligations is the causal theory. According to this account, people come to have duties to children because they create them in a needy state and effectively make profound choices on their behalf.

I then consider the extent to which these parental obligations entail a duty to promote children's well-being according to the theory developed in Part II. I show that existing approaches to parenting in a liberal society either permit parents to pass on beliefs which harm their children or imply that children will receive inadequate guidance about ethical matters. In place of these existing theories I defend perfectionist parenting, according to which parents have a direct moral duty to promote the best views of ethics to their children.

I conclude Part IV with a discussion of the duties non-parents might have to children. I consider evidence which suggests that parents matter less for children than is commonly assumed and that other members of society matter more. I suggest that this influence on children generates duties to the children that are similar – albeit weaker – to those of parents.

Part V: Distributive Implications

In the final part of the book, consisting of two chapters, I consider the implications of the theory for two of the most significant practical debates concerning children. First, I defend the principle of fair equality of opportunity (FEO) in education funding. In particular, the claim that wealthy parents should be barred from transferring resources to their children, which seems inconsistent with the priority view defended in Part II. I show an argument for equalizing opportunity flows from my account of children's well-being. I argue that children's social relations with one another are dependent upon FEO and, in particular, upon children interacting with the world as agents. This means that their lives take the shape they do because of their own actions and abilities. Secondly, in Chapter 14 I make the case for 'parental subsidies', meaning that parents should receive money for the state to support their efforts caring for their children. I justify such subsidies because they make the project of raising children more attractive and this option benefits both parents and non-parents. The latter benefit from having the viable option of being a parent, with viability meaning that becoming a parent does not mean impoverishing oneself and giving up other valuable goals.

PART I

Children and Moral Theory

1

The Aims of a Moral Theory

This book is a work of normative theory – I ask how children *ought* to be treated, not how they are in fact treated right now. This subject matter implies that most of the book is focused on assessing various arguments of moral philosophy concerning children's rights and duties. The aim of the exercise is to put forward a theory of justice for children that systemizes our moral intuitions across different cases into a coherent whole – a process John Rawls termed *reflective equilibrium*. The result is an account of how a just society would treat its children.

Before thinking through these substantive arguments, I make two points on methodology. First, that the work is primarily a piece of *ideal theory*, meaning that the central issue is what a fully just society looks like and especially how such a just society would treat its children. I do not consider, except where relevant, the separate question of how current societies should be changed to become more just, nor do I consider the serious political and social barriers that must be overcome to better achieve my conception of justice. While an ideal theory is necessarily incomplete, in this chapter I explain the vital importance of ideal theory against important objections to this. Secondly, I consider the value of empirical work, particularly from the social sciences, to normative theorizing. I argue that while normative and empirical enquiry are logically separate, there are powerful reasons for political theorists to refer to research in sociology and political science when developing principles, even when working on an ideal theory. In my view, a concept of children's well-being cannot be determined without some discussion of what factors contribute to their development, a partly empirical question.

Ideal theory

An 'ideal theory' is one which aims to paint a picture of what a fully just society would look like. It contrasts with a non-ideal theory, which offers practical guidance about what a person should do right now, given their society's situation and political prospects. Rawls suggested that the central way in which theory becomes 'ideal' is if it assumes that all citizens will act justly. To illustrate, a socialist ideal theory would imagine a society in which all citizens act according to the laws and moral principles that perfect socialism. The role of the theory is working out what socialism would look like, not what would be the best way to achieve socialism given current concerns. Such an account is idealistic because it assumes away various contingencies that might be threatening to the achievement of the specified conception of justice, for example that people will only work when financially incentivized or will set up black markets. A non-ideal socialist theory would be one that gave guidance on how socialism could cope with potentially disruptive actions.

While often discussed as a binary concept, it is better to view the ideal/non-ideal distinction as a scale. A theory is extremely idealistic if seemingly deep features of the human condition (like the fact that people sometimes engage in selfish behaviour or that there is widespread political disagreement) are assumed away. On the other hand, a theory would be only modestly idealistic if it assumes away some contingent features of current economic or political circumstances that are likely to change soon. Contemporary political philosophy has been dominated by theories which are relatively idealistic along this spectrum. Rawls' own *Theory of Justice* aims for what he terms a 'realistic utopia'. His basic model is to accept certain features of human nature and human society as given, but to assume a society in which everyone is committed to a liberal egalitarian theory of justice. Some theorists have gone even further, defending conceptions of justice they readily admit are in some sense impossible for humans right now (Cohen, 2009). What matters to them is to show what the best way to live together would be, absent the constraints of human nature.

While dominant in the literature, ideal theorizing has been subject to several related critiques. The most common is that by idealizing away challenges, a theory risks becoming irrelevant to contemporary society, and thus ideal theories fail to provide any useful guidance (O'Neill, 1987; Farrelly, 2007; Jaggar, 2009). In different ways, these critics argue that 'an account of justice must give due consideration to the diverse complexities that arise in the real world' (Farrelly, 2007: 862). For instance, theories of distributive justice go awry if they assume away the deep financial difficulties that arise when trying to protect and promote rights, since such idealizing assumptions will mask the serious trade-offs that must be faced when attempting to achieve justice in non-idealized circumstances. A theory that assumes away real-world constraints is of limited use to those tasked with making tough economic decisions, which seems highly problematic given one might think that guiding decisions about how to promote justice is a central purpose of a political theory.

However, while this kind of reasoning shows that normative theories are not entirely composed of ideal theories, it does not necessitate a wholesale rejection of the latter. There are many different types of political and ethical problems. While some of them do indeed require practical non-ideal solutions, others can only be properly addressed by a more idealized theory. Perhaps the core purpose of a more ideal theory is to provide a yardstick by which to judge any given set of alternatives; this is termed the 'evaluative' function of justice (Gilabert, 2011). A further related role of a more ideal theory is to clarify people's moral duties even when we know they will not meet them, because to do otherwise is to 'let them off the hook' (Stemplowska, 2008: 339). Fulfilling this evaluative function of ideal theory is the central contribution of this book, and crucially this evaluative function does not depend upon the ideal being achievable right now or perhaps ever. While prescriptions of justice depend on feasibility, evaluations do not (Gilabert, 2011: 52–63).

The worry with abandoning ideals because they are judged to be 'unfeasible' is that this will allow powerful individuals or groups to determine not merely what will actually happen, but also what morality requires of them. Imagine a society in which one group occupies all positions of power and does so in a way that is resistant to all possible social change. In such a depressing society there are no feasible social changes at all. It is thus hopelessly idealistic to hope for a more equal distribution of power and privilege. Faced with such a society, the 'realistic' theorist should take the fact of injustice as an assumed feature of the world and try and work out what's best to do *given* the injustice. There is great value in such a theory, but it is also vital not to let the oppressors off the hook by pretending that the situation is a just one.

In this book, I will defend moral principles that condemn many ingrained features of current societies. In particular, I suggest that some of the cultural patterns of behaviour that create children's early environment are highly detrimental to their well-being. I suggest that many parents and others are morally blameworthy for the conditions of children's upbringing. While I do not provide a map for alleviating these sources of injustice, recognizing them as injustices and showing who is morally responsible are highly important endeavours. As such, my theory is an example of why the evaluative mode of theorizing is an important, but incomplete, part of normative thinking and one that is not undermined by questions of feasibility.

Methodology and the relevance of social science

While this book is a work of moral theory that develops abstract normative principles, it draws on contemporary social science more than some normative political theorists believe is necessary or useful. An influential challenge to using empirical evidence comes from philosophers who believe that arguments about moral principles cannot depend upon factual premises. This sharp distinction between facts and values descends (principally) from the work of David Hume; he argued that empirical considerations can have no intrinsic normative force. Empirical research can describe the character of the world around us, but it cannot tell us whether this world is good or bad, just or unjust. Even seemingly clear social problems, like the number of children living in severe poverty in rich societies, are not themselves evidence of any injustice or wrongdoing. Rather, these facts provide evidence of injustice only in virtue of a moral principle – for instance, that every child is owed a basic standard of living or that inequalities between people should be the result of choices rather than chance.

More recently, G. A. Cohen has argued that the defence of principles of justice must be divorced from empirical considerations. Cohen's target is theories (like John Rawls') that develop principles of justice in response to 'facts' about human nature, society or practical possibilities. A consequence of Rawls' approach is that, if the facts were found to be different to those he supports, then the principles of justice that depend on these facts would have to be revised. In this way, many political theorists suggest that our moral views about justice should be sensitive to our beliefs about the world or about human nature. In contrast, Cohen argues that moral beliefs cannot be challenged by facts in this way, instead 'a principle can reflect or respond to a fact only because it is also a response to a principle that is not a response to facts. To put the same point differently, principles that reflect facts must, in order to reflect facts, reflect principles that don't reflect facts' (2003: 214).

To illustrate Cohen's point, consider a moral principle that seems to directly reflect a particular set of facts, perhaps that schools should be run locally rather than by a centralized national system. This argument puts forward a claim about what justice requires – 'schools should be run locally' – that seems dependent on empirical claims, specifically the evidence of locally run schools' better performance. If this evidence were shown to be incorrect then someone who believed schools should be run locally should abandon that belief. However, while this argument appears to be sensitive to empirical considerations, the core moral principles do not depend upon the contingent facts of the case. The moral principle in play is that 'the government has a moral responsibility to promote children's interests in the most efficient way possible'. This more general principle is not fact dependent. The *implications* of the principle do depend on empirical considerations, but not the *content* of the principle. According to Cohen, arguments against this moral principle can instead only be based on different normative principles, perhaps that all children should have the same standard of education, or that parents' moral rights must be respected even at a cost to efficiency.

However, while I do not deny Cohen's views about the logical relation between facts and principles, I do suggest that there are reasons why, even in this approach, empirical research is relevant to the *formulation* of principles as well as to their *implementation*. Moral and political philosophy are centrally concerned with people's duties to one another and understanding the contents of those duties requires comprehending people's needs and interests. Specifying those interests depends upon features of human physiology and psychology. In Part II, I develop an account of what constitutes 'children's welfare'. This account necessarily draws on empirical research about what effects different actions have on children's development, citing the findings of psychologists. Evidence like this is essential to working out whether a given action or event is good for a specific child and for children more generally.

Concepts like well-being are thus fundamentally composed of both empirical and normative aspects which cannot be neatly separated. Empirical evidence from the social and natural sciences are necessary parts of working out what makes for a flourishing life, but one cannot know what is in children's 'best interests' just by looking at relevant scientific data. There will inevitably be trade-offs among the promotion of different skills and aspects of well-being, and no empirical theory can provide guidance about these. Science might in principle tell us precisely how much different types of upbringing would affect a child, but it could not possibly answer which was *better for them*. Knowing the answer to this question depends on knowing what kind of qualities are good for a person to have and, more deeply, what kind of person it is good to be, and these are fundamentally moral questions.

Therefore, well-being is an instance of a concept which necessarily draws together insights from many disciplines, including moral theory, psychology, and social and natural sciences. To the extent to which these concepts are central to a theory (as they are to mine), there are good reasons to pay attention to both empirical and normative research when forming a view. Thus, while I concur with Cohen that moral theory and the social sciences are logically distinct, a theory of children should be sensitive to current research on how children behave and what social practices currently exist regarding their care, even if this means that the arguments put forward are in some ways contingent on this empirical picture being accurate.

2

What is a Child?

Before developing a theory of children's justice, it is worth first exploring the question of what it means to be a 'child' and why the category of childhood matters. According to the law in most Western countries, to be a child just means to be a young person below the age of about 16 or 18. For the purposes of my theory I will mostly follow this simple age threshold definition. Defining childhood just in terms of age might seem overly simplistic for a philosophical theory, which we might feel should provide a more nuanced account of childhood. One apparent weakness of thinking only about age is revealed by the extent to which 'the age of adulthood' varies dramatically in different times and places (Aries, 1962).[1] This societal variation illustrates that whatever features of childhood we take to be special, there will be no clear point at which we can neatly differentiate the category of adults from the category of children.

A more fundamental challenge to a purely age-based definition is that by itself age seems a morally irrelevant distinction. The mere fact that one person is 17 whereas another is 12 or 30 does not seem to tell us anything about their moral status or their interests. Rather, what matters is the physical, mental and social ways that children differ from older people. In a broad sense, differences in *capacities* are what meaningfully differentiate children from adults. But the problem is that there are no capacities which neatly track a person's age. This is most obviously true when we think about people who are very near in age to one another, but either side of the supposed dividing line. Nothing much changes physically or mentally on the day of one's 16th or 18th birthday, or even in one year. Therefore, the class of 'children' becomes highly arbitrary.

While it may be true in the aggregate that young people have less developed cognitive or physical capacities than older people, this is not true in every case. The media is rife with stories of 'child prodigies' who are capable of feats well beyond that of most adults. Absent these somewhat anomalous cases, the cognitive capacities, political acumen and intellectual maturity of many teenagers are equal to or greater than those of some adults. Therefore, the line between 'child' and 'adult' will necessarily be somewhat arbitrarily placed and, worse, there will always be many people either side of the line with similar capacities to people on the other side. Such persons might seem to be wronged by the age threshold. Imagine someone who is 15 but is in all cognitive respects as capable as someone who is 20. Treating this person as a 'child' – by denying them the vote or various legal powers – appears disrespectful and groundless, given what should matter is their own abilities, not the average of people their age.

Sometimes, it is indeed highly important for the state and other institutions to have a fine-grained understanding of any one child's capacities. For instance, in custody battles, the expressed preference of a child should override the legal authorities' views of what is in their 'best interest' if, and only if, there are good grounds to treat the child's decision as properly autonomous (Mullin, 2014). In such cases our treatment of young people should align with the state's treatment of adults, who are permitted to make all kinds of decisions that the state believes to be against their best interests, even where there are grounds to think that the adult is mildly cognitively deficient in some way. Thus, when deciding whether to let children's preferences override their objective interests, it is vitally important that relevant actors understand the maturity and capacities of *a particular child*. Some 12-year-olds have the kind of stable preferences that should count as an autonomous will, whereas others do not, and the treatment of these children should differ because of this.

However, in many other cases there are powerful reasons to stick to the simpler age-based criteria. A person's age is an easy trait to measure whereas more nuanced categories like 'capacity', 'competence' or 'autonomy' are often hidden and subject to widespread disagreement. Developing institutions that have fine-grained knowledge to assess the capacity of each child might thus be impossible, given the depth of information this would require. At the very least it would be prohibitively costly. Further, it is often important for justice that people are subject to publicly understood and verified rules (Williams, 1998). Treating everyone under a certain age as a child meets this publicity criterion, whereas rules that judge, for example, some 15-year-olds as adults and others as children because of slight differences in capacity might not be.

Secondly, as I have argued elsewhere (Fowler, 2014), there are often powerful reasons of justice to treat all young people of the same age similarly in the political sphere. For instance, there are good reasons to think that all children should get the vote at the same age even though capacities differ among children. While it might seem that because the only reason children should be excluded is a lack of capacity, and therefore that capable children should be able to vote, a purely capacity-based criterion would imply that some children would get the vote much earlier than others and would thereby enjoy more political power over the course of their lives. Giving all children the vote at the same age preserves a valuable kind of equality among them. This kind of argument applies to many other kinds of legal powers and to treatment by various institutions like the school system. In sum, while the category of child is undoubtedly complex, there are good reasons, both practical and substantive, to use the simplistic definition by age as the starting point for a theory of justice.

Why is childhood special?

As I have suggested, what really matters about childhood are the aggregate differences in capacities between older and younger people. Here I consider which differences in capacity are particularly salient and why they matter for a theory of justice. While there are many such differences, the most important are that children are lacking in cognitive capacities to the extent that they are not fully autonomous and that they are necessarily inexperienced such that they require role models or guidance on how to act. For these reasons, among others, the most important features of childhood are that children are highly *malleable* and are extremely *vulnerable*. By malleable, I mean that the beliefs, values and practices held by a child are in flux and that differences in their childhood are highly significant in guiding their later decisions and their future.

Given the broad nature of these claims, I will not delve into describing the specifics of how and in what ways children's cognitive capacities underpin their vulnerability and malleability in as much detail as would be required by a work of child psychology or sociology. Here it is enough to note that no plausible theory could doubt that children are both vulnerable and malleable in the sense I mean. Seeing children as intensely vulnerable merely recognizes that while they are babies or toddlers who must be under constant care to survive, and for many years afterwards, children are less physically able than adults and lack the requisite experience to navigate social situations. Children's malleability is demonstrated by the obvious extent to which growing up in a particular cultural context shapes their expectations, values and beliefs. Later in my theory it will be important to tease out whether this effect is due to their parents or to their peer groups, but clearly some combination of parental and social circumstances has great impact.

Focusing centrally on children's lack of autonomy and other capacities will strike many as inappropriate, since it seems to miss the many things which children are capable of and thus treats childhood as 'deficit' (Matthews, 2008). It is worth stressing there are many things that children might be comparatively better at than adults, for instance learning a second language. And indeed, as I noted there are some contexts, such as medical care or custody disputes, when it is important to recognize that even young children are capable of some autonomous actions (Mullin, 2014). However, while these concerns are significant and must inform our overall understanding of what childhood is and why it matters, I believe there remain good reasons to focus on the 'deficits' of childhood for the purposes of a theory (though I do not suggest that being vulnerable to others is a 'deficiency', properly understood). Vulnerability and malleability are highly significant features of childhood because they mean children are particularly affected by the actions of others. I suggest that liberal theories of justice often understate the extent to which these features matter and thus that it is worth building a theory which takes these more seriously. To say this does not imply that vulnerability or malleability are the *only* features of childhood – just that they are important enough to demand attention from a theory of justice. My theory is not presented as a complete theory of childhood, only as a discussion of the way that children fit into an established set of liberal political theories. Within this context the most important features of childhood are the ways in which children lack experience and cognitive capacities.

Further, while my theory is relatively neutral between contested theories of child development, it is worth noting that children's lack of experience is not just a function of their diminished physical capacities, rather it exists because they are people at the start of their lives. My theory takes the temporal aspect of childhood to be definitive of what it means to be a 'child'. Even though we can say someone is 'like a child' if they possess some childish quality or, in extremis, have the cognitive capacities of a child, they are not really thought of as *a child*. It might be that some of the most normatively interesting aspects of childhood are driven precisely by someone's lack of experience. Suppose that people came into the world as cognitively and physically developed adults, but that nevertheless they had no knowledge of their surroundings or understanding of the world. Such newborn adults would still be intensely reliant on older people to explain the world and what they must do to function in it, and we might guess that they would be highly likely to be socialized into the values and practices of the community of which they are a part. In this way, my theory need not rely on a picture of children as being radically cognitively impaired. Rather, while I do take diminished cognitive and physical capacities to be definitive of childhood – and part of what makes childhood special – lack of experience is also a central element of why children must be treated as a separate category by theories of justice. In sum, I take what many have argued to be a problematic approach by treating childhood as centrally interesting because of children's extreme vulnerability – an approach that often sees them treated them as patients rather than agents (though this becomes less appropriate as children grow up). I do not do this because vulnerability captures all of what matters about childhood, but because it matters enough to deserve sustained theoretical attention.

Why children's deficits matter

Children's vulnerability matters in lots of ways for politics. Most obviously, the fact that children are incapable of providing themselves with food, shelter and other basic goods means that society must have a way of effectively ensuring that their basic needs are met. Beyond basic physical needs, children need special care, attention and guidance if they are to flourish. These needs create a political issue in so far as we need to know how much care children are owed and who should bear the costs of such care. There is controversy about the extent to which procreators should be required to pay for childcare and education, or whether all of society needs to fund childcare for reasons of justice or efficiency. In either case, the existence of children undermines a simple conception of people as independent economic actors who should have whatever resources the market allows them. For a large stretch of everyone's life they were unable to earn resources in the market yet required resources to survive. Children's vulnerability shows the extent to which all of us depend on others for our very survival, and the extent to which the differences between those who prosper and those who do not depends on choices made for, not by, those people.

Children's malleability matters because it pushes questions of socialization to the fore. Children come into the world without any values or understanding of how to act and thus need to learn behaviours and ideals from others around them. Sometimes children's lives – both while children and later as adults – are much worse than they might have been because of the kinds of things they have been socialized into believing are valuable goals or are expected of them. This feature of childhood means that those with whom children come into contact have enormous power over their lives. Philosophically, the relevance of childhood is that many actions which seem only to affect the agent him or herself become other-regarding. Many of our mundane actions must be subject to moral scrutiny because of the subtle but profound ways our choices and actions affect children; the collective impact of many adults creates an environment that make it more likely children will believe the ideas that those adults promote or act in similar ways to them. It is these questions of socialization and influence that my theory will chiefly address.

Note

[1] An extreme case is suggested by Basden who writes of the Ibo children in Nigeria 'from the age of about three years, the Ibo child is reckoned as sufficiently advanced to be left more or less to its own devices. It begins to consort freely with children of its own age or company (otu) and to take its share in work and play' (1966: 65).

PART II

A Distributive Theory
for Children

3

The Currency of
Children's Justice

In this chapter I discuss the appropriate currency of children's justice, meaning what things count towards saying one child is advantaged or disadvantaged relative to another for the purposes of justice.[1] While the question is abstract, it is one that confronts policy makers as well as theorists. For instance, the goal of equalizing children's 'life chances' has been a theme of recent political discourse in the United Kingdom.[2] Making sense of this aspiration requires an account of what life chances are and how to assess whether two children have equality in this respect. Broadly speaking, there are two leading answers to the currency question. Resourcists believe that justice is about the distribution of all-purpose goods which contribute to people's ability to pursue their plans, welfarists believe that justice must be concerned more directly with how well people's lives are going. In this chapter I defend welfare as the appropriate metric in the case of children. While versions of resourcism often work very well in the case of adults, they fail when applied to children.

Two bad answers: measuring money and happiness

Here I briefly discuss two popular but unpersuasive answers to the currency question. According to the money view, the right metric of justice is material resources. People who have more wealth or income are advantaged relative to those who do not have such resources. The happiness view counts being advantaged or disadvantaged in terms of subjective mental states. People who feel 'happier' are better off than those who do not. While both these accounts have been influential in policy frameworks, each must be rejected.

The problem with the money view is that it misses far too many things that seem relevant to assessing a child's relative situation compared to others. Consider the following example:

Inequality: Two children, Alan and Bill, live in households with equal wealth and income. However, Alan lives in a smoggy area that causes him to become ill, he is generally neglected by his parents and his teachers do nothing to encourage his interest in art or music. Bill has excellent health, an excellent quality of care and a school that provides him with extensive extra-curricular activities.

Given the differences in their lives it would be absurd to conclude that the two children have similar levels of advantage. Bill's situation is preferable to Alan's, and he has these advantages *because* of the different impact of social institutions. This example shows that an adequate theory of children's justice must assess things beyond access to monetary resources and instead take a more holistic view of the effects of institutions and practices.

This analysis might suggest that the happiness metric is more appropriate because it counts anything that makes the person feel sad or unsatisfied as relevantly disadvantageous. However, this standard is also inadequate: to see why, consider this variant on inequality:

Inequality entitlement: Alan and Bill's respective situations are the same as before. However, Alan comes to accept his situation and even believes that people like him deserve to be worse off than others. Bill comes to think he deserves an even more fortunate life. Alan reports himself as being satisfied, whereas Bill reports himself as unsatisfied.

The subjective happiness measure wrongly concludes that under these conditions Bill is worse off than Alan. In the philosophical literature, Alan would be referred to as an example of someone who holds an 'adaptive' preference, that is, their preferences are shaped by conditions of injustice such that the person comes to want the injustice to continue.[3] While there is current debate on how to respond to adaptive preferences in practice – sometimes overriding someone's wishes is disrespectful and paternalistic – it seems vital that a metric is at least able to count people like Alan as being disadvantaged in an important way. The problems subjective measures of advantage have with adaptive preferences are especially acute in the case of children. Children's malleability makes them prone to accept their conditions as normal or acceptable. As such, a vital role for a theory of children's justice is to show how people who come to accept their injustice have been wronged by this upbringing.

John Rawls: primary goods

A more sophisticated theory of advantage is provided by Rawls' 'primary goods' metric, defined as being 'things that every rational man is presumed to want'. Rawls writes that 'For simplicity, assume that the chief primary goods at the disposition of society are rights and liberties, powers and opportunities, income and wealth' (1999: 62). Rawls also argues that what he terms 'the social base of self-respect' is 'perhaps the most important primary good', and that things such as health and intelligence count as primary goods, although they are less controlled by society (1999: 62). In this way, this metric can assess the effects of social institutions on people's lives in a much more comprehensive way. The core idea is that social justice is concerned with the distribution of basic goods that all citizens want because they are vital for their success in whatever plans they have.

Just as with the simple income metric, the primary goods approach is not concerned with how a person chooses to spend their resources, only with the amount of resources they have available. Justice is about giving each person a fair share of primary goods, not about assessing how well different people are using their share. Rawls writes, 'it [the primary goods measure] does not look behind the use which persons make of the rights and opportunities available to them in order to measure, much less to maximise, the satisfaction they achieve. Nor does it try to evaluate the relative merits of different conceptions of the good' (1999: 94).

While it remains one of the dominant views in the literature, the primary goods approach has been subject to several important critiques. Two related problems are sufficient to show that this metric cannot work in the case of children: (i) it misses relevant components of what constitutes advantages for children; (ii) people have different capacities to convert primary goods into a flourishing life.

The first problem is advanced by Colin Macleod, who offers a case in which two children have equal shares of primary goods, and their basic needs are met, but where one 'has a secure and loving family and is exposed to a rich range of opportunities for imaginative play, adventure and aesthetic exploration and experience', whereas the other lacks these (2010: 80). He suggests that since the things enjoyed by the first child are not primary goods, there is no real divergence in the levels of advantage enjoyed by these children. This case shows that while primary goods is a broad metric, it cannot capture everything that is relevant when assessing a child's level of advantage. There, according to Rawls' metric, are many things whose distribution is affected by social institutions, but which cannot plausibly be understood as 'resources', which matter for children. Having fun or adventures are aspects of what we think of as a 'good' childhood, and whether children have access to them does seem relevant for justice.

The second problem for Rawls is that people have different abilities to utilize primary goods. This objection to primary goods is made by Amartya Sen, who writes that 'People have disparate physical characteristics connected with disability, illness, age or gender and these make their needs diverse' (2000: 70). This implies that two people who have equal shares of primary goods cannot always be treated as if they have the same level of advantage. While Sen's examples are important, they do not exhaust the differences between people's capacity to effectively use resources to improve the quality of their lives. The ability to utilize primary goods is influenced by one's character, skills and personality and by the nature of one's projects. Since these are shaped during one's malleable childhood, it follows that the ability of a person to flourish given a fixed level of resources will be greatly influenced by the circumstances of their childhood. The implication should be that children who convert resources inefficiently *because* of their upbringing are counted as disadvantaged by that upbringing. To illustrate, consider the following:

Waste: Callum and Danielle are young adults with identical shares of primary goods. Callum lives in a community which devotes itself to worthwhile and valuable pursuits. Danielle lives in a place in which people spend a great deal of time and money building a huge hideous monument. All of Danielle's friends and family contribute to the pointless monument and all (mistakenly) think that it's of vital importance to keep building it. She also dedicates herself to this worthless pursuit.

While they have the same level of resources, Danielle's life becomes much worse than Callum's and the central reason is the social context into which she was born and in which she was raised. The effect of her upbringing has been to make her more likely to pursue a worthless project. In Part III I explore whether ensuring Danielle becomes autonomous is likely to protect her from being socialized into valuing worthless pursuits. At this point it is enough to say that a metric of advantage must at least be open to the conceptual possibility that a child can be disadvantaged because he or she is socialized into preferences that cause him or her to flourish less than other children.

Ronald Dworkin and the envy test

The problems with Rawls' approach might be resolved by a different resourcist view: Ronald Dworkin's. The core of Dworkin's theory is what he terms the 'envy test'. Envy is here used in a technical sense: a person envies another if she or he would be willing to swap their bundle of resources for her or his own. To illustrate, consider two people with different preferences on housing. Emily loves living in central London and would hate to live in a smaller city or in the suburbs. Felicia likes living in a large space and doesn't mind the location. Emily can only afford a small flat, whereas Felicia can have an enormous house. While their resources are very different, neither person envies the other, and this implies the two have equal levels of advantage. For Dworkin, the envy test compares both a person's access to material resources and their personal resources, which includes any physical or mental attributes that they and others value. The implication is that things like physical strength or a good memory count as resources that must be weighed against material goods when comparing people's overall level of advantage.

Dworkin's view is well placed to deal with the inequality example. In this case, Bill has everything that Alan has plus other goods. Alan can thus be presumed to envy Bill in the Dworkinian sense. Note that Alan may not envy Bill in the emotional sense (he might well not think about Bill at all or be glad about Bill's good fortune) but this is irrelevant. Conversely, Bill would not be willing to swap his bundle with Alan's. Since both parties prefer Bill's bundle of resources, the envy test correctly judges Bill to be advantaged relative to Alan. Further, this judgement would not be affected if we imagine that Alan has grown accustomed to his bad lot or that Bill demands an even better one, as in the inequality entitlement example.

As well as providing positive arguments in favour of a resource metric, Dworkin offers a powerful argument against the welfarist alternative – *the expensive tastes objection*. Dworkin asks us to imagine a man, Louis, whose welfare depends on his having access to the very finest things in life. If he can't get these things Louis becomes morose and sullen. The welfare metric counts Louis as badly off because he is unable to get the special items he likes. More significantly, it treats him as badly off, even if he has exactly the same amount of money as any other member of society, because other members are happier with cheaper goods. This inequality of welfare produces perverse consequences if it is used as input into egalitarian or other left-leaning accounts of justice. Suppose that a state wanted to equalize Louis' welfare with that of another person. The only way to do it would be to provide him with significantly more resources that he can then use to buy more expensive items, up to the point at which the welfare of the two is equalized. Dworkin believes that this conclusion is extremely unfair, 'Louis should be free ... to make the best sort of life he can with his fair share of social resources. But he should not be free to trespass on the fair shares of others, because that would be unfair to them' (1981a: 238).

Like other resourcists, Dworkin's approach is about distributing useful goods to people, not in judging how they spend them. Here he promotes a powerful argument in favour of this kind of approach because it avoids subsidizing expensive tastes. Provided Louis has the same amount of resources as everyone else then we should judge his level of advantage as being the same. He is at liberty to spend his share on expensive goods, but if he ends up with less enjoyment or welfare because of his own decisions about how to spend these resources he is not worse off from the point of view of justice.

However, while Dworkin's account is powerful when applied to adults, his view still fails to provide a good measure for assessing childhood. The resources model again cannot deal with the effects that childhood has on people's later use of their resources. Consider:

Diet: Graham and Harry grow up in different parts of a multicultural society. The two men have identical jobs and earn equal amounts of money. Both enjoy the cuisine most common in the area in which they grow up, and in each case the cuisine is part the cultural heritage of which their respective parents are members. Both men get equal enjoyment from eating, but neither can stand the diet preferred by the other. Graham's diet is salty, fatty and lacking in vegetables, whereas Harry's diet is extremely healthy. Over time Graham's diet leads to some serious problems.

Suppose that because of his diet, Graham will have to spend a good deal of his resources on medical treatment and will still have worse health outcomes than Harry. Since both men get the same amount of enjoyment from their diet, Harry seems to be better off overall than Graham. Nevertheless, according to Dworkin and his followers this is not an inequality that ought to count for the purposes of justice. Like Louis, Graham has an expensive taste. He does not *envy* Harry in the relevant respect, since he could eat the same food as Harry and pay nothing in medical bills. However, unlike Louis, Graham did not actively cultivate this expensive taste. Rather, both men like the food that they ate as children and which is enjoyed by their friends and families. While it is, of course, possible for people like Louis to intentionally cultivate particular preferences, this process is not the normal one of preference formation. Rather, our own experience of life is that many (perhaps most) preferences are formed by a complex process of choice, habituation and social expectation. The result is that those things we come to like and expect as children will have important consequences for later choices, and this method of acquiring preferences seems significantly different from the atypical case of a person who goes out of their way to cultivate a new desire.

Dworkin and his followers do accept that there is a potential problem with his theory when people have preferences for things which do not promote their welfare. However, they only recognize this when people live under circumstances of injustice (e.g. Parr, 2018). Here, Dworkin discounts preferences which are formed due to other people's wrongdoing as such preferences can be treated as special cases and ignored. However, in the diet example, Graham and Harry do not acquire their preferences due to an injustice. Rather, they acquire them because of the mundane processes of socialization, which explain a large part of ordinary behaviour. For this reason, it is not plausible to count Graham's preference as a special case for the theory that can be evaded and treated differently. It is cases like Louis', in which a person goes out of their way to cultivate a preference, that are anomalous. Therefore, I believe there is no way to escape the conclusion that Dworkin's resource theory will count Graham and Harry as having the same level of advantage since they have the same amount of resources and merely choose to use them in different ways. This conclusion thus sees their experiences in childhood as being equally good, or at least not disadvantageous. But this conclusion is not correct, instead we have reason to hope that the more children have upbringings that promote healthier living, the more this will enable them to live better and healthier lives.

Just as with Rawls' view, the overriding problem with the resourcist metrics is that how people use their resources is also something justice should care about, especially when everyone's differing decisions are influenced by social institutions and practices. The resourcist answer looks viable when people can be assumed to have stable and autonomously formed beliefs and desires. The problem in the case of children is that these qualities are not best regarded as *inputs* of the theory of justice – facts about people that the theory must take account of – rather they should be regarded as *outputs*. What preferences, values and abilities a person comes to have are determined in large part by the way that they are raised, which in turn depends upon the norms and institutions which govern their society. The effects of upbringing on children's later values, habits, characters and preferences must itself be a central part of how a theory assesses different social arrangements.

Sen, Nussbaum and capabilities

These problems for resourcists prompt a move to the welfare approach, which aims to directly measure how well a person's life is going. We count a person as advantaged when his or her life is going well and disadvantaged when it is going poorly. On such a broad metric enjoyment and play will count as sources of advantage for some children relative to others. Welfarism can capture inequalities caused by differences in socialized preferences and thus provides a building block for assessing the justice of different social practices in this respect.

The initial step in developing a well-being view is defining what counts as a life 'going well'. This task is challenging in at least three respects. First, there is just the sheer complexity of human life. No theory could possibly rank all the possible ways of living in a diverse liberal society. Secondly, there is the problem of disagreement. People disagree significantly about what constitutes living well and this implies that many citizens will not agree with the ethical assumptions guiding any specification of well-being. Finally, well-being views face the problem of responsibility. It is important to distinguish a case when someone *chooses* not to enjoy a good life from one in which they did not have the option of having it at all.

The most famous welfarist view, the capability theory of Martha Nussbaum and Amartya Sen, is a potential answer to these problems. The approach understands well-being as the real freedom to achieve valuable ends or 'functionings'. The theory tries to solve complexity by homing in on a few functionings that are seen as most important. The widespread agreement on the value of these functionings answers the diversity challenge while the theory incorporates responsibility by valuing the capability to do something rather than the action of actually doing it. Thus, a person who chooses to forgo a good is not relevantly disadvantaged. The capability view has been explored as a metric of justice across many contexts, including children's justice (for instance, see Hartas, 2014 and Schweiger, Graf and Cabezas, 2016).

The capability view relies on measuring valuable functionings. People's lives are better or worse depending on their real freedom to access things on this list. Given the complexity problem, such a list is unlikely to capture all valuable goods. However, the hope is that the protection and promotion of some centrally important functionings is sufficient to adequately measure people's relative advantage. Nussbaum has suggested the following list, which I will use as a starting point for my own theory:

1. **Life**. Being able to live to the end of a human life of normal length; not dying prematurely, or before one's life is so reduced as to be not worth living.
2. **Bodily Health**. Being able to have good health, including reproductive health; to be adequately nourished; to have adequate shelter.
3. **Bodily Integrity**. Being able to move freely from place to place; to be secure against violent assault, including sexual assault and domestic

violence; having opportunities for sexual satisfaction and for choice in matters of reproduction.

4. **Senses, Imagination, and Thought**. Being able to use the senses, to imagine, think, and reason – and to do these things in a 'truly human' way, a way informed and cultivated by an adequate education, including, but by no means limited to, literacy and basic mathematical and scientific training. Being able to use imagination and thought in connection with experiencing and producing works and events of one's own choice, religious, literary, musical, and so forth. Being able to use one's mind in ways protected by guarantees of freedom of expression with respect to both political and artistic speech and freedom of religious exercise. Being able to have pleasurable experiences and to avoid nonbeneficial pain.

5. **Emotions**. Being able to have attachments to things and people outside ourselves; to love those who love and care for us, to grieve at their absence; in general, to love, to grieve, to experience longing, gratitude, and justified anger. Not having one's emotional development blighted by fear and anxiety. (Supporting this capability means supporting forms of human association that can be shown to be crucial in their development.)

6. **Practical Reason**. Being able to form a conception of the good and to engage in critical reflection about the planning of one's life. (This entails protection for the liberty of conscience and religious observance.)

7. **Affiliation**. A. Being able to live with and toward others, to recognize and show concern for other human beings, to engage in various forms of social interaction; to be able to imagine the situation of another. (Protecting this capability means protecting institutions that constitute and nourish such forms of affiliation, and also protecting the freedom of assembly and political speech.) B. Having the social bases of self-respect and non-humiliation; being able to be treated as a dignified being whose worth is equal to that of others. This entails provisions of non-discrimination on the basis of race, sex, sexual orientation, ethnicity, caste, religion, national origin.

8. **Other Species**. Being able to live with concern for and in relation to animals, plants, and the world of nature.

9. **Play**. Being able to laugh, to play, to enjoy recreational activities.

10. **Control over One's Environment**.
   A. Political. Being able to participate effectively in political choices that govern one's life, having the right of political participation, protections of free speech and association.
   B. Material. Being able to hold property (both land and movable goods) and having property rights on an equal basis with others;

having the right to seek employment on an equal basis with others; having the freedom from unwarranted search and seizure. In work, being able to work as a human being, exercising practical reasoning and entering into meaningful relationships of mutual recognition with other workers. (Nussbaum, 2000: 78–80)

Many of these functionings, like life or health, are uncontroversial and would form part of any plausible account of what makes a human life go well. These and many others are not upheld only or distinctively by the capability view, since resourcists such as Rawls or Dworkin have other arguments to show why it is good for people to be able to have the right of political participation or a right to personal property. Nussbaum's list more clearly moves beyond resources through those items which track mental states or things with intrinsic value, like access to nature or emotional development. While assessing what counts as 'good' emotional development is a highly difficult task, this criterion, at least in principle, allows Nussbaum's metric to adequately capture a much broader range of threats to children's relative advantage than can resourcist views, for instance that the conditions of their upbringing cause them needless sadness or loneliness.

Modifying the capability view for children

Central to the capability view – the reason it measures *capabilities* – is that people who fail to take up an opportunity should not be thought of as disadvantaged. A person who fasts still has the capability to eat, whereas the person who cannot afford to eat does not. Measuring capabilities, rather than achievements, is vital to allow for people's free will and to ensure that they are not thought of as disadvantaged by their own choices.

While this approach seems attractive in the case of adulthood, it opens the capability approach to a similar problem to that identified with resource views. Namely, it understands people only as autonomous choosers, which is a false assumption for part of their lives, since everyone goes through childhood. As a result, the capability theory may be poorly placed to deal with cases in which a person's flourishing is impaired by the circumstances of their upbringing.

To illustrate this worry, consider the case of girls who drop out of education early because of social pressure. Some believe that this shows the advantages of the capability approach over resourcist views (Berges, 2007: 19). The capability approach supposedly counts such young women as disadvantaged, since they lack the real freedom to access education.

However, this depends upon the means by which they are prevented from accessing school. If their parents or communities banned them from going, then it seems clear that the girls are indeed disadvantaged; however, more sophisticated resourcists will also be able to count girls in such situation as lacking in the same kind of way. A more difficult case is one in which the girls experience social pressure to stay at home but no direct coercion. That is, if there is a general expectation that 'success' for girls consists in becoming a housewife, whereas success for boys depends on other kinds of attainment, including success at school. This expectation might manifest in the ways that children's parents and family friends praise their actions. The worry with this subtler kind of obstacle is that it becomes difficult to say when the girls lack the capability to achieve education and when they have the capability (the option of going to school) and choose not to use it.

The right way to respond to this concern is for our measure of advantage to directly count the goods that people achieve. Here my approach mirrors those of other authors who have applied the capability theory to children (see Walker, 2006; Peleg, 2013). In different ways, these theorists suggest that in the case of children we directly measure their *achievement* of valuable functionings, in this instance we measure the relative advantage of the girls and boys by directly counting the amount of education they access. Any barriers that prevent girls from being educated, whether societal or institutional, make them worse off. Measuring achievements directly is justified because children are not yet autonomous; as such, we can presume that the girls are not yet capable of making a responsible choice to forego education.

This suggests the following hybrid view of advantage. For adults we measure capabilities, and thus conclude that people are not disadvantaged by things they choose not to pursue. For children we measure functionings directly. However, even this hybrid model will not do because cultural or familial pressure that occurs during childhood can cause people to disadvantage themselves when they get older. Suppose a case where the state forced all children to go to school till age 16, but once they reached this age all girls chose to leave education and did so because of their commitment to cultural practices they had been inducted into during childhood. This loss of later well-being is at least potentially something that should count towards assessing how well their childhood promoted their interests, especially if the girls do not count as fully autonomous persons.

The answer, I suggest, is that we assess the advantage provided by childhood via measuring its effects on the goods persons receive as children and any effects on the later achievement of (not merely opportunity to achieve) a good as an adult. The point is that if an adult turns down a good thing because of their childhood then this loss of flourishing should be seen as a cost of that upbringing to that person.

Capabilities and neutrality

The second issue to raise with respect to Nussbaum's list is that she believes it is neutral between competing 'conceptions of the good' or views about what a good human life requires. Neutrality over ethics is the central divide within liberal theory that I raised in the Introduction. Some liberals believe that principles of justice must not favour any view of ethics over another. For Nussbaum and also for Sen the capability approach is neutral because the relevant list of functionings is at such a high level of generality all people can see the value of the good in question. Sen writes: 'Capability reflects a person's freedom to choose between alternative lives (functioning combinations), and its value need not derive from one particular "comprehensive doctrine" demanding one specific way of living' (1999: 118). The implication is that the list of goods provided by Nussbaum is intentionally vague, such that there are many different ways of fleshing out each component. Later in the theory, I will argue that her list is too unspecified to provide a plausible view of what justice for children entails. However, making this modification requires revealing problems with the principle of liberal neutrality, which will be the topic of Part III. For now, Nussbaum's list is sufficiently clear to show the advantages of a view that picks out the objective components of well-being, rather than either subjective happiness or a measure of resources, but I will further modify this list to provide a better metric in later chapters.

Conclusion

In this chapter I have outlined several possible metrics of justice and I have rejected various resourcist accounts. While different in many respects, these views all fail because important questions of justice are raised in relation to how people use their resources. This cannot be merely thought of as a personal choice, but rather is deeply affected by their upbringing. I also rejected subjective measures of well-being, since people's beliefs about their own well-being are often unreliable, particularly given that their preferences adapt to injustice. In their place I defended the welfarist view and tentatively defended Nussbaum's list of valuable capabilities as a guide for what counts as valuable. The latter is sufficient to flesh out the initial building blocks of my theory in the rest of this part of the book, but in Part III I show how this list grants a more attractive theory of justice for children if the aspirations to be neutral about the good are rejected and justice is understood as the project of creating an environment in which children are likely to adopt worthwhile and valuable ways of living.

Notes

[1] Terming this question the 'currency of justice' follows Amartya Sen (1987).

[2] See https://www.gov.uk/government/speeches/prime-ministers-speech-on-life-chances, or Field (2010).

[3] For discussions of adaptive preferences see Jon Elster's discussion of sour grapes (1983: 26). For discussion of their political implications see Rosa Terlazzo (2015: 206).

4

Welfare across the Lifespan

In this chapter I discuss the different ways that childhood can contribute to a flourishing life. First, there are the *intrinsic* benefits of childhood; a happy and contented childhood contains more goods than a sad one and the person whose childhood was happy probably has a better life because of this. Secondly, childhood has *preparatory* or instrumental benefits, things that add value because they confer later benefits when the person becomes an adult. While childhood makes both intrinsic and instrumental contributions to a person's flourishing, there has been debate about the relative importance of these different effects. Some have argued that children lack the ability to access many of the most important components of flourishing, such that a good childhood is mainly about preparing for a flourishing adulthood. Others have argued that childhood is itself the site of distinctive values that are essential for a good life and that an overly preparatory childhood leaves a person impoverished.

In response, I argue that while the intrinsic and preparatory benefits of childhood can certainly conflict, the tension between them has been overstated. Many of the most important goods are things which we access through a combination of actions and events that happen during our childhood and adulthood. The gradual and intentional development of one's talents and powers confer value independently of the achievements that these talents allow, and relationships which persist over a long time gain special importance. This view shows why childhood is an essential and intrinsic part of a good life but one whose value is not reduced merely to fun or play, which are the widely discussed examples of intrinsic goods of this stage of life.

Childhood and flourishing: the predicament view

Proponents of the predicament view suggest that childhood is a regrettable state to be in. A modest version of this thesis is that a period of childhood, say a year, is worse for a person than a similar period of adulthood, while a strong version is that childhood is an actively bad state. Both versions imply that childhood provides at best a relatively small direct contribution to the value of a life, and the implication is that childhood's main contribution will be through its effects on adulthood. The justification for the predicament view is that a person's access to the most important human goods depend upon them having adult-like qualities and capacities and that since children lack these capacities it follows that they must lead a less flourishing life.

Tamar Shapiro argues that being a child is about lacking autonomy, which matters for flourishing because only autonomous beings can take responsibility for their actions in a way that gives these meaning and value. Children lack the ability to be agents in this sense because they lack a stable character that can generate an authoritative will. According to Shapiro, 'the condition of childhood is one in which the agent is not yet in a position to speak in her own voice because there is no voice which counts as hers' (1999: 729). While children can make choices and take actions, they cannot take moral ownership of these actions and thus they cannot realize the distinctive human good of agency.

On Shapiro's account, childhood is analogous to other kinds of cognitive impairment that hinder a person's ability to act autonomously. This analogy offers support for the predicament view because other ways in which a person might become non-autonomous are generally seen as being very bad for that person. A brain injury that reduced someone's cognitive powers to those of a young child would be a serious harm. Similarly, even those sympathetic to animal rights usually accept that animals cannot achieve the level of well-being that is possible for humans because they lack autonomy.

Aside from autonomy, there are several other valuable functionings which children cannot access fully. Children generally lack knowledge about important political and social matters. They also have a tendency to trust people in unqualified ways that leaves them particularly vulnerable given the world they actually inhabit (Hannan, 2018: 12–16). While some argue that children's innocence is a valuable feature of their lives, in dangerous contexts, like the ones many children often face, innocence is not a good way to approach matters. Finally, children often lack the ability to succeed in long-term complex projects (Slote, 1983: 14). For instance, the artistic work of the average ten-year-old child would not usually count as an impressive achievement if created by an adult, suggesting that children's limited creative powers do not allow them to produce things of the same objective value as adults.

The intrinsic goods of childhood

In response to those who argue that childhood's benefits are mostly instrumental, several theorists have contended that childhood is a phase of a person's life that makes a large direct contribution to their flourishing (Macleod, 2010; Brennan, 2014; Gheaus, 2015). One reason is that childhood can be a happy time and it is uncontroversial to claim such positive emotional states are at least somewhat valuable for both adults and children. Brighouse and Swift add that many of these positive emotions are things which children can enjoy more readily than most adults. They write:

> the capacities to feel spontaneous joy, to be surprised, and to be thrilled seem to diminish a good deal with age: while they are valuable in adulthood as well as in childhood, it may be unrealistic to expect them to be experienced with great intensity much beyond childhood but entirely realistic to think that many children can experience them fully. (2014: 65)

Their suggestion implies that childhood's usual contribution to the flourishing of an overall life is to allow people to access enough of these types of emotional goods since most are unlikely to experience them later in life. Brennan and Macleod (2017) go further and argue that there are goods which people can *only* realize while children. Their examples include unstructured play, which is fun and enjoyable for children but less significant for adults, and innocence about sexuality, which has a cost to adults but is important for children. If they are right then childhood is even more central to flourishing, since a purely preparatory upbringing would guarantee that people miss out on some valuable things.

Therefore, one way in which childhood might be special is that it allows access to some goods not readily available to adults. Another possibility is that things which are bad for adults are not bad for children. Consider the hierarchical relationship between a child and his or her parents. Children are highly dependent on their parents and are often taught to be deferential to them. These features suggest a relationship of domination, implying that one party is subject or beholden to the other. If both parties were adults, this relationship would be one characterized by severe inequality and injustice. But this kind of status hierarchy might only be problematic because it is bad *for adults* to be part of hierarchical relationships. Children's diminished cognitive faculties make dominating them acceptable or even desirable. The harm of domination occurs because it disrespects the agency of the other, but children cannot be disrespected in this way. Brighouse and Swift suggest that

> children have a right to be treated paternalistically. If, as we have claimed, children have weighty interests in both well-being and future agency, interests that depend for their realisation on their not being free to do as they will (run into the road, eat too much junk food, skip school), then respect for those interests itself demands that others act paternalistically toward them. (2014: 70)

Macleod (2010) argues that it is precisely the inequality in children's relationships that allows them to access some of the distinctive goods of childhood, that children's innocence about the state of the world allows them to sustain a 'carefree' attitude which is often either impossible or inappropriate for adults because of their responsibilities.

Taken together, these various arguments suggest that the best way to integrate childhood into the overall theory of well-being is to use different lists of goods for people's interests when they are children and when they are adults. These lists are fused because, over a whole life, persons have interests in achieving things on both lists. On this model a flourishing childhood is an essential component of human flourishing, since people who miss out on the goods of childhood will always be lacking some elements of a fully flourishing life.

Testing the two views

These two sets of arguments paint very different pictures of childhood's value. According to the first, children are held back from flourishing by a lack of valuable capacities, on the other the innocent and carefree attitude of childhood is an important component of a valuable life. Here I consider various thought experiments to test which of the two pictures is most plausible. Building on a suggestion made by Brennan (2014: 37), Patrick Tomlin offers the following case:

> **Deprived of Childhood**. Dane is given pills to speed up his development. Aged 6, he is physically and mentally a fully-grown man. (2016: 35)

If childhood were a burdensome state, then we ought to think that what has happened to Dane is a good thing. He has replaced a decade or so of childhood with a decade of adulthood, which is a better state to be in. But instead it seems Dane has missed out on something vitally important – a childhood. Part of our belief that Dane has been harmed is driven by the social context, the ways that others will treat him and react to him. But more fundamentally we can explain the belief that Dane has been harmed by appealing to the intrinsic goods of childhood; he is missing out on things like unstructured play and carefree innocence. While he will get more of the goods of adulthood these are not sufficient to compensate for the loss of the goods he could have had.

As such, Tomlin's 'deprived of childhood' example is evidence against the predicament view. However, Tomlin then raises the mirror case to show why the counter view is also problematic:

> **Left as a child**. Erin is given pills to prevent her becoming an adult. Aged 55, she continues to be a child, both physically and mentally. She is well cared for. (2016: 35)

If being a child is better for the person than being an adult, then we ought to think that Erin is made better off by the pills. More modestly, if a year spent as a child is just as good for someone's well-being as a year of adulthood, then Erin is left no worse off. However, neither of these judgements appear plausible as Erin seems to have been seriously harmed. Again, part of our judgement about this case can be explained the social context; people might relate differently to a child they know to be 55 even if such a person is physically and mentally indistinguishable from a younger child. However, these social differences cannot fully explain our intuitive reactions to this case. Rather, we believe that remaining a child is very bad for the person and therefore that Erin is being seriously harmed by the pills even if everyone interacts with her in just the same way as they would with any other child (Lomasky, 1987: 202).

Taken together, Tomlin's cases suggest something of a puzzle. It appears that we believe that being denied a childhood would be bad, but that remaining a child would be bad as well. This set of beliefs is difficult to explain by any set of assumptions about the relative value of one year of adulthood vs one year of childhood. A different possible explanation is that both Dane and Erin are missing out on a *diversity* of goods (Gheaus, 2015: 17). This suggestion looks promising since over their lifetimes Dane and Erin each access a set of values that is less diverse than those acquired by a person who has experienced both childhood and adulthood. However, while promising, this consideration cannot fully explain our judgements about these cases. The problem is that there is a very large variety of goods that can be experienced *within* adulthood or childhood. An adult can have periods where they live in hedonistic excess and later live in asceticism, can work both as a banker and a schoolteacher. The fact that there is a wide diversity of goods available to adults is problematic for the diversity of goods argument in two ways. First, it means that having a flourishing childhood is not necessary to access a variety of different goods. Dane could miss out on all the goods of childhood but then go on to experience a very diverse range of things in adulthood. Since Dane would thereby access a wide variety of goods, it remains unclear how we can explain the judgement that Dane is made worse off by missing out on childhood. Secondly, reflecting on the possible diversity of goods open to adults casts doubt on the belief that having a variety of goods would necessarily be better than enjoying the same good in a more sustained and focused way. Imagine someone who decides at a young age that they would like to be a teacher. They take steps to reach this goal as a child, and then work as a teacher for 50 years until retirement. They do this all in the same city. While this life might not be to everyone's tastes, it does not seem seriously lacking in the way that both Dane's or Erin's lives are. Thinking about these cases suggests both are missing out something more fundamental than simply a diversity of experiences.

Lifelong goods

What I term 'lifelong goods' are valuable things which can only be accessed by a combination of experiences during different stages of life. Their value comes from the narrative connection between experiences or processes over time and from the way that projects or relationships change and develop over longer periods. The result is that the persistence of a project or relationship across different life stages creates a distinct value over and above the value of each composite element. An example of a lifelong good is a friendship that one makes during childhood and continues during adulthood. In part, such friendships are valuable because they cumulatively provide lots of happy experiences over time. I suspect though that when we reflect on such relationships we feel that their value is considerably greater than the mere accrual of good experiences would suggest; instead, these different experiences gain added value through the shared experience of long periods of change and development. Intimate relationships that span this process of development give each party the experience of being a source of influence upon the other. Another paradigmatic example is the parent–child relationship; typically, parents will care for a person from the moment of his or her birth, will gain intimate knowledge of him or her as a young child and will continue this relationship into adulthood. Noting the importance of lifelong goods thus explains the special importance of the parent–child relationship to both parties, even after the child has grown up. The bond is special not just when the adult is caring for the child, but afterwards too, because the experience of being cared for in this way connects current experiences to things that happened in the past when both parties (but especially the child) were very different.

The category of lifelong goods helps explain the intuitive belief that both Dane and Erin miss out on something vitally important by not experiencing many values of this kind. Neither will have relationships with people of similar age that persist across changing life stages and both will miss out on features of the usual parent–child relationship. Dane does not have a childhood in the normal sense. While he has biological procreators, these people will never care for him while he is a child. Perhaps if all people were like Dane there would be no category of 'parent' at all, since what parenting means is so bound up with the care of children. Even if he does have parents in some sense, his relationship with them cannot be informed by their shared knowledge of his growth and development and his parents' causal role in his life's story. For him these things happened immediately and were not part of an interactive process. In a different way, Erin misses out on important features of this relationship. Since she will forever remain a child, she lacks the change and development which is central to lifelong goods. While we can presume that she has close and caring relationships with her parents, these relationships will not develop into ones in which she and her parents can relate to one another more directly as equals.[1] For many people, moments when a child demonstrates the development of her cognitive or physical capabilities (e.g. the first time a person rides a bike without stabilizers) are moments of great value and importance and we must assume that Erin will have many fewer of these as she ages.

Both parties also lose lifelong goods that accrue during the development of talents and abilities. We must assume that Erin will never gain the level of skill acquired by trained adults since the development of skills is part and parcel of the cognitive development that characterizes the transition to adulthood, which, for Erin, is blocked. While Dane can learn to master new skills and abilities up to the usual limits of adults, he lacks the experience of taking something up as a child and continuing it as an adult. The case of Dane tells us something about why the claim that children's creativity lacks value is misguided. What is valuable is not just the end achievement, but the process of learning and growth that made that final achievement possible. If the ability to produce art was just given to someone by a pill it would be much less special than the ability that has been honed for years, starting at a young age.

Therefore, noting the distinctive value of change and improvement helps make sense of our feelings about Dane and Erin. We can see why both are badly off, without suggesting that childhood is better or worse per se than adulthood. This insight shows that much of the existing literature has been formulated in a misleading way. The mistake is believing that the right way to think about the contribution of childhood to flourishing is to compare the value of a year of adulthood to one of childhood. To illustrate this methodology, consider these remarks by Tomlin:

> [I]magine, at the end of their lives, we could give people a pill which ensured that they had a period of ten years or more where their mental and physical capacities deteriorated into those of children. Would we give people that pill? It seems doubtful, to say the least ... Why imagine that inferior intellectual and physical ability is a personal tragedy at the end of a life, but the boon at a beginning. (2016: 8)

Tomlin believes that the fact we would not give this pill is a strong reason to believe that being a child is worse than being an adult. However, once we see the importance of development to flourishing, we see that Tomlin's inference is unwarranted. There seems ample reason to think that the gradual development of abilities from initial wayward steps as a child to the sure steps of a master is a valuable process that confers well-being over and above the value of each instance of creation. In contrast, the gradual loss of creative powers seems intuitively much worse for the person, a slow inability to achieve things which used to be possible. This explains why years of diminished capabilities at the beginning of a life might be good for the person, since it allows for the value of growth, whereas years of similarly diminished capacities are bad at the end of a life. Lifelong goods can thus show why both childhood and adulthood matter for flourishing and why the *order* of goods matters to the generation of lifelong goods.

The shape of a life thesis

My arguments thus far, and particularly that the order of a person's experiences matter over and above whether those experiences are good or bad, will seem to some readers to imply that I take an unpopular view in what is known as the 'shape of a life' debate. This discussion asks whether and why the distribution of well-being within a life matters over and above the value of each stage. Broadly speaking, we can distinguish two kinds of lives based on the distribution of well-being within them. An 'upward-sloping' welfare curve refers to lives that start out with low levels of well-being and later gain higher levels, while downward sloping refers to the reverse case. A number of theorists argue that shape matters, that is, that when welfare comes in a life might have added value, and they tend to argue that upward-sloping distributions are good things to have whereas downward-sloping curves are negative (e.g. Campbell, 2015). The consensus among theorists working on this question matters because it implies that the best shape of life is achieved by people with preparatory upbringings. Preparatory upbringings yield upward-sloping curves since these give the person a relatively bad childhood but a better adulthood. Thus, my acceptance that the order of goods matters might also seem to commit me to thinking that preparatory upbringing is better. Here I show why shape does matter but not in a way that disrupts my view.

To illustrate the basic appeal of the view that upward-sloping lives are good, Dorsey calls to attention the character MacKendrick from the TV show *Mad Men*, who has a terrible accident shortly after a moment of great personal triumph. Dorsey believes that this accident seems even worse because it comes after a period of great happiness and success. In contrast, if we imagine the mirror case, in which a person suffers a terrible accident but later has huge success, then the life led seems much better. While the events are the same their order seems to matter (2015: 304). Others note our emotional reactions to periods of loss in our own lives, suggesting that most people feel especially bad about becoming worse off than they once were, a reaction against a downward-sloping curve (Glasgow, 2013: 668).

However, while these psychological reactions exist they are not sufficient to show that upward-sloping curves are always better than downward ones. Instead, this psychological reaction of loss might be grounded by the fact that the loss did not seem inevitable, at least not at that time. Consider a person who has had a bad breakup. Their sense of loss might reflect the fact they had thought, at least at some point, that the relationship could have been a longer or more successful one. They might be sad about the way that things eventually turned out, not the order of their moments of happiness. Further, there are some countervailing considerations which seem to matter psychologically. Good phases of life that happen early give us longer happy memories, which might extend their contribution to well-being. A person who has had an extremely happy childhood has a lifetime of good memories, whereas a person who has an excellent time in retirement has many fewer. These remarks are far from conclusive, but they do suggest that our intuitions are often very contextual and unclear and cannot ground the general presumption that upward-sloping curves are better than downward ones.

More significantly, there is a better theory that can account for our intuitions regarding the best shape of a life. This is the *relational view*, which holds that moments of life gain in value when they relate to each other in valuable narrative ways. For instance, early hardships that lead to later success have a valuable narrative relation to such success. The early sacrifices are given meaning and structure by the later triumph. According to this proposal,

> the shape of a life is a sign of and is thus a signatory valuable indicator of the existence of important narrative relations between a life's significant events, relations that constitute the achievement or failure of long-term projects or the fulfilment of or the failure to fulfil valuable long-term goals, and so forth, and which help to determine the contribution of these events to the overall quality of a life. (Dorsey, 2015: 313–14)

According to the relational view, what really matters is whether and how people succeed in their long-term aims. This will often coincide with an upward-sloping welfare curve, because success in one's projects brings greater well-being as we age. The person who decides to pursue a career might make sacrifices to further that end (lowering their well-being), then succeed and enjoy their success (raising their well-being). The reason this person seems to have had a good life is not because of the upward-sloping nature of a graph of their well-being, but rather because their success was achieved by their own actions. What adds value to individual moments of happiness is when the order of the events in someone's life reflects and expresses some feature of the person rather than a 'disordered sprawl of incidents' (Clark, 2018: 373).

Unlike the view that upward-sloping curves are always intrinsically good, the relational view does not necessarily provide any reason to favour a preparatory view of a 'good childhood', since doing better in adulthood than childhood tells us nothing, in itself, about the value of the life in question. What will add value to a life is giving children the ability to pursue their own interests and to form relationships with whomever they choose. This kind of supported freedom gives roots to later projects which will add value and is the beginning of a process of self-discovery. Thus, lifelong goods are at the core of how a life may have value over and above the value imparted by each of its moments. Therefore, while the literature on the shape of life thesis might have seemed a challenge for my view, instead the best view from this debate can be incorporated into it.

Conclusion

In this chapter I have discussed the relationship between a person's childhood and other stages of life. I argued that the debate thus far has missed the importance of lifelong goods, whose value depends upon progress and change throughout both adulthood and childhood. I have shown how this insight explains why we intuitively know that people can be disadvantaged by missing out on either childhood or adulthood. In so doing, I rejected both the predicament view and views that hold childhood is directly good mainly because it is a stage filled with fun and play. Fun is important but the contribution of a childhood to a good life is much more profound than that. The arguments of this chapter suggest that we should not understand the valuable functioning described in Chapter 3 as a list of things that a person can have at any one moment. Rather, fully realizing most values requires a purposefully driven series of connected events over time. These considerations show that childhood is directly integral to the well-lived life and that the best way to further this value will be to give children the means to control their own lives when possible, the space to develop their own pursuits and relationships and a context in which early projects and relationships can be pursued into adulthood.

Note

[1]   In considering the case of Erin it is important to note that there are people who 'remain children' in the sense of never attaining the cognitive or emotional capabilities possessed by most adults. A consequence of my view is that such relationships do lack valuable features of other parent–child relationships, but of course they nevertheless have great value.

5

Priority, Not Equality, of Welfare

In this chapter I consider which distributive principles should guide justice for children. An initial starting point to the analysis is that there is *moral equality* between all, regardless of their race, gender or their parent's position in society. Moral equality implies that each child's interests should be counted equal by principles of justice, and thus that there are no children whose interests should be favoured just because they are members of some special group or occupy a particular social status. Making this basic assumption of moral equality may seem to imply a demanding principle of distributive equality. We might think that because children have equal claims of justice, the morally best society is one in which children live equally good lives. However, I will reject this more demanding requirement of equality because of what is known as 'the levelling-down objection'.

After rejecting distributive equality, I consider the two leading alternatives: the sufficiency and priority principles. Sufficiency requires that each person gets 'enough' of whatever is to be distributed, priority that special emphasis is placed on ensuring benefits go to those who are worse off. I defend the priority approach but show that there are often instrumental reasons to pursue equality and sufficiency within this framework. The implication is that justice for children requires promoting the welfare of all children, but with a strong focus on the interests of those children whose well-being is lowest.

Distributive equality

The principle of distributive equality has great intuitive appeal, perhaps most of all in the case of children. Equality is especially attractive for children because they are not responsible for their quality of life. Many believe that the industrious should earn more than those who work less hard, but whatever the merits of this view it cannot apply to young children who are not yet responsible for their choices. For this reason, it is consistent and plausible to think that justice demands equality among children, even where one thinks justice permits large inequalities among adults. However, while this view has great intuitive force, it is not a useful guide to what justice ultimately requires.

Before revealing the problems of distributive equality, it is worth clarifying what precisely this view entails. While there are many principles that are fairly described as being 'egalitarian', here I limit my discussion to principles which assign *intrinsic* value to distributions in which people have equal levels of advantage. Intrinsic value here refers to properties which make a distribution good in itself, whereas instrumental value refers to things which are good because they promote some other value. There is powerful evidence to suggest that equality of income or wealth has large instrumental benefits, for instance that equality promotes social trust, lowers crime and raises health outcomes (Picket and Wilkinson, 2009). Inequalities can also lead to differences of social status or the domination of one part of society by another (Scanlon, 2003). These provide powerful instrumental reasons to favour equality, but they do not show that equality is intrinsically important.

There has been some debate about whether the discussion over the intrinsic value of equality has any significance. Martin O'Neill writes:

> Why should it be in itself bad for inequality to exist? … the sheer variety of ways in which inequality is non-intrinsically bad demonstrates precisely why we have such good reason to eradicate inequalities where this is possible. If on the other hand we accept claim A [the intrinsic account of egalitarianism] the ideal of equality can seem unduly obscure and abstract, as a merely *arithmetic* goal, the value of which is impossible to grasp. (2008: 123–4)

He goes on to argue that the instrumental reasons surveyed are both sufficiently powerful to ground egalitarianism and the only things the canon of historical egalitarians ever cared about.

O'Neill is right to stress the force of the instrumental case for equality, and my own account will later rely on precisely such considerations, but he is wrong to infer that there is no practical importance in the more abstract question of whether equality has intrinsic value. There will often be cases where many or all the instrumental reasons do not apply and in those instances there is no reason to equalize children's outcomes unless equality has intrinsic value. Importantly, the instrumental reasons to favour equality are often absent when the relevant metric is welfare rather than resources. Resources are both rivalrous (people have interests in the same resources) and transfer directly into power over others. People with economic resources are often able to dominate or exploit poorer people in the marketplace, but there is no comparable way in which people who have flourishing personal relationships or artistic success can dominate those with lower levels of well-being. Therefore, it will often be true that the instrumental case for equality does not apply when thinking about welfare. If these instrumental reasons are the only things that press for equality, then there will sometimes be no grounds to equalize well-being. Alternatively, if the initially plausible case for distributive equality stands, then there will be always be some reason to try to equalize children's well-being. As such, showing whether and when the intrinsic case for equality fails is significant for understanding what justice for children requires.

The levelling-down objection

Levelling down occurs when a change makes a situation more equal but no one any better off. Derek Parfit (1987) believes that *all* egalitarian principles must favour levelling down to some extent and that *any* principle that favours levelling down must be rejected. He therefore argues that once the levelling-down issue is considered, equality can play no intrinsic role at all in considering what justice requires. To illustrate the issue, consider two possible ways that a society might be organized. Each of these possible societies is of equal size and within each society there are three equally sized groups of children. Term these the badly off, the middle and the best off (see Figure 5.1). For ease of analysis, assume that a child's welfare can be captured numerically, such that a child with welfare of 10 has a life which is twice as good as that of a child with a welfare of 5.[1]

In Society 1 there is perfect equality welfare across all social groups. In Society 2, the best-off children enjoy a standard of welfare which is significantly higher than that of worst-off. A purely egalitarian distributive principle thus evaluates Society 1 as being significantly better than Society 2. A hybrid principle might not have this implication: our evaluation will depend on the relative weight of equality (where Society 1 scores highest) vs total welfare (where Society 2 scores better). However, any hybrid principle must judge that Society 1 is better in one respect because it is more equal.

The problem is that every single person in Society 2 is better off than their counterpart in Society 1. That's what makes this case an instance

Figure 5.1: Levelling down

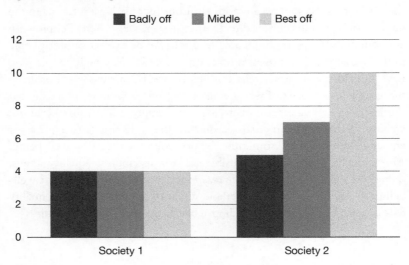

of levelling down: no person has benefited by the creation of equality. There is a legitimate debate to be had about whether small gains to the worst off outweigh large losses for those better off, but a case where no one benefits is not levelling down in the technical sense. Parfit argues that justice is about promoting the interests of persons and that there can never be a reason to make some people worse off without showing how some others benefit. I concur with Parfit's judgement about this case and we can strengthen his reasoning by considering other examples:

New park: The young residents of Birmingham and Manchester have no access to outside spaces. Spending so much time indoors means that these children don't spend much time with friends. The two groups of children have equal but low levels of well-being. A philanthropist donates money to build a park on condition all the money is spent in Birmingham. Birmingham accepts the donation and from then onwards children in Birmingham experience a higher level of welfare than those in Manchester.

Building the park system has created a welfare inequality between the two groups of children but due to the restrictions of the donation there is no way to give every child these advantages – the only way to preserve the initial situation of equality is to decline the money and thereby to level down. Parfit's point is that there are no good reasons to want to level down by refusing the money since it makes some children's lives better and does not affect the lives of the others in any way. The importance of this stylized example is to show how our intuitions about helping the worst off can sometimes mislead us. While often the best way to help the worst off is to take resources away from those who are better off, via taxation or redirecting social spending, sometimes it is not. The new park example is an instance where these two aims come apart, when achieving equality does nothing for the worst off and, significantly, the intuitive attraction of distributive equality falls away.

Sufficiency

Sufficientarianism is defined as the belief that 'what is important from the point of view of morality is not that everyone should have the same but that everyone should have *enough*' (Frankfurt, 1987: 21–2). This requires that the state use 'available resources in such a way that as many people as possible have enough, or in other words, to maximise the incidence of sufficiency' (Frankfurt, 1987: 31). This ideal of sufficiency has considerable intuitive plausibility and is a standard which can be fruitfully applied to many areas of policy-making that affect children's lives. A common understanding of parental rights seemingly relies on a sufficiency standard, since so long as parents do a good enough job promoting children's interests they should retain custody (Shields, 2016). As I discuss in more detail in Chapter 13, a number of theorists endorse a sufficiency principle about education, according to which inequalities of schooling are permissible so long as every child reaches the same minimum standard (see Anderson, 2007; Satz, 2007).

Applied to the theory developed in Chapter 3, sufficientarianism requires that each child reaches a relevant threshold of well-being where that is understood as achieving the objective list of functionings. The distributive principle assigns a disvalue to any person not meeting this threshold, meaning that distributions in which lots of people do not meet the threshold are worse than distributions in which only a few do not have enough. According to Frankfurt, the sufficiency view is indifferent to inequalities above the threshold, so in this instance the only aim of distributive justice is to minimize the number of people who do not enjoy a high enough level of welfare. The resulting theory of children's justice can cope with the problems outlined for distributive equality. The sufficiency principle only ever requires redistribution when this moves someone above the relevant threshold and as such there is no reason to take from those who have more if this does not benefit someone badly off. Thus, in the new park example there is no reason to take away the benefits that accrue to children in Birmingham since this does not improve the condition of anyone in Manchester.

However, despite these attractions, sufficientarianism is subject to serious problems. The first is that all the plausible metrics of justice, including the ones I rely on, are scalar not binary in nature. This means they are things that a person usually benefits by having a little more of, rather than there being a clear line between people living 'good' or 'bad' lives. This sets up a spectrum on which people at one end lack all the components of flourishing and have very poor lives, while people at the other end possess lots of valuable functionings and live excellent lives. Between these two poles are many different possible positions in which people have some of the dimensions of flourishing in varying degrees. This leads to an inability to easily demarcate 'good enough' from 'bad' lives and this is a serious problem for defenders of the sufficiency principle since they must provide a good reason why a particular point on the scale of well-being is a threshold that matters significantly for justice. The sufficiency standard creates a huge moral difference between people who are just below the threshold (who are owed aid as a matter of justice) and those just above (who are owed nothing).

In addition, even if defenders could find such a rationale for placing a threshold at one point rather than another, an even more serious issue is that some inequalities above the threshold *do* seem to matter for the purposes of justice. Consider the following case:

Dispersing disadvantage: A society consists of only two groups. One group of children can expect to live extremely happy and flourishing lives. The other group have lives which are a bit better than 'good enough' but significantly worse than those of the first group. Now imagine that the situation of this society changes and that one group of children will have to have some of their advantages taken away. If the reduction happened to the best-off group, they would still be better off than the others. If it happened to the worst-off they would be reduced to the level of just having 'enough'.

The sufficiency principle is indifferent between these two options since neither will move anyone below the sufficiency threshold and therefore, according to Frankfurt, neither choice would be unjust and neither more just than the other. All that matters is whether anyone falls below the threshold. However, in this example Frankfurt's view does not seem plausible: while the worse-off children might still have 'enough' after their loss it is deeply unfair to take things away from them to protect the advantages of children who are much better off.

These problems, among others, have led some writers to conclude that the sufficiency approach is a dead end. However, other political philosophers have defended a more limited role for sufficiency and their arguments are instructive in showing how sufficiency is part of what justice for children requires, even if it cannot be the whole story. These theorists show that caring about the sufficiency threshold does not mean there is no reason to care about people above it (Shields, 2012). Instead, we can think that the priority of justice is to ensure everyone has enough goods to live a decent life, but once this goal is secured other distributive principles, like equality, come into play. This proposal is not vulnerable to the problems exposed by the dispersing disadvantage example, since it can accommodate the intuition that fairness requires taking advantages away from the extremely well-off children.

Another way to save the sufficiency approach is to suggest this kind of principle works best when applied to the distribution of specific goods, rather than an overarching metric of advantage like welfare or resources. While there is no good way to define what counts as 'enough' welfare it is relatively simple to set a threshold of goods like food or shelter. For instance, men require about 2,500 calories a day to remain in good health and women 2,000. Above this threshold, additional calories do little good and eventually become harmful by contributing to weight gain and obesity. A person's interest in having more food is a *satiable* one, very powerful up to a point but then it quickly falls away. Because our interest in food is satiable, a principle which requires that all people have enough food but is indifferent to people's access above this level seems highly plausible.

While many of our interests are not fully satiable, there may be similar points at which our interests in some things become much less pressing. For instance, a person with no close friends or a partner might well be extremely lonely and miss out on an important component of flourishing. Creating and sustaining one flourishing relationship will add a great deal to their well-being. Conversely, a person who has three or four close friends gains much less from a new friendship. Their interest in having friends may not be quite satiable but, with three or four, comes fairly close to being satisfied. Similarly, as I will discuss later, several theorists believe that many people have a powerful interest in becoming a parent (Brighouse and Swift, 2014). But a person's interest in becoming a parent to one or two children is usually much greater than his or her interest in parenting more children than this. For this reason, the best way to promote total welfare might well be trying to ensure that each person reaches the threshold of each of the various components of well-being. This shows why sufficiency principles have been useful to theorists working across many policy domains. Ensuring children have 'enough' care, health care or education makes sense as part of a theory of distributive justice, but these aims are not best explained by an overarching requirement that they have 'enough' welfare.

Priority

The priority principle states that benefits which accrue to the worst-off matter more than those which accrue to the better off. Unlike the equality principle it holds that that benefits are always valuable. If possible, benefits should be given to those who are currently worse off, but it is still a good thing to benefit those more fortunate.

In operation, the priority principle requires knowing how much well-being will go to each person under a possible distribution and then assigning a multiplier based on that person's current level of advantage. To illustrate, suppose there is a non-shareable good that must go either to Graham or to Harry. If Graham gets it his well-being will increase by 10 units, but if Harry gets it his will improve by 20. If the only aim is to maximize the total well-being, then obviously we ought to give the goods to Harry. However, Harry is already well off whereas Graham is badly off. We judge that this means Harry has a multiplier of 2, whereas Graham a multiplier of 5. The total moral good of giving the benefit to Harry is thus 40 (2 × 20), whereas the value of giving it to Graham is 50 (10 × 5). Thus, the priority principle would favour giving the benefit to Graham because he was so much worse off to begin with.

Priority is not just a reflection of the fact that there are diminishing marginal returns to many goods. It might well be that giving benefits to the worst off is more efficient than giving to the already advantaged. The same amount of money might buy one person essentials like housing, whereas in another case it would merely buy more luxuries which contribute much less to welfare. This effect is true and highly significant for distributive justice, but the central claim of the priority view is that fairness, as well as efficiency, means that benefits that accrue to the worst-off matter more.

This moral priority often has practical importance, especially when it is not easy or efficient to help the worst-off children. Consider the case of children with costly medical conditions or those requiring significant social care by the state. If our aim is simply to maximize aggregate well-being across all children then it may be that this care would be unjustified since the same money could produce bigger gains by helping many more (better-off) children in easier-to-achieve ways. However, on the priority view children with substantial needs would receive an extremely large modifier, such that relatively small benefits to them nevertheless generate large returns from the perspective of justice. The priority principle thus gives reasons to help the worst off beyond efficiency.

On the other hand, according to the priority principle there is always also some reason to benefit more-advantaged children, so levelling down is never required. A concern for the worst off sometimes means favouring equality, but when there are ways of helping the worst off that require inequality these will be permissible. To give some examples from later in the book, some of the central drivers of children's welfare are time spent with their parents and friends and the ability to explore valuable pursuits. There are things that the state can do to better enable children to access these goods, for instance by paying for leave for parents or by providing free access to music or sports facilities. Regrettably, though, it will often be difficult to ensure that these benefits flow to the worst off. In such cases, the provision of these benefits will exacerbate an existing welfare inequality. Nevertheless, provision of important goods to many children is a large, and unqualified, good. The priority view can explain why, but also why it would be even better to enable children who were not already advantaged to access these goods.

Conclusion

In this chapter I have argued that the priority view is the most attractive principle of distributive justice. Inequalities matter a great deal only when they cause some to become worse off. Material inequalities will often, though not always, have this effect in a market economy, but other kinds of inequality do not license problematic forms of domination or exploitation. I also argued that often the best way to promote well-being involves a sufficiency standard of certain goods. Clear examples include ensuring children have enough food, shelter and medical attention, but it is also plausible that there is a similar threshold with respect to more complex constituents of welfare such as personal relationships or creativity.

Note
[1] It is obviously impossible to measure welfare (understood according to the capability view developed in Chapter 3) so precisely.

PART III

Perfectionism and Upbringing

6

The Case against Neutrality

In this chapter my aim is to show why the leading arguments in favour of liberal neutrality fail and are particularly problematic in the case of children. As we saw at the end of Part II, developing a metric of children's flourishing is hindered if it is impermissible to take a stand on contested ethical questions. Here I argue that there are no good grounds to justify the neutrality restriction. In the ongoing argument these discussions create the space for a perfectionist theory of upbringing. According to such a theory, children are owed an environment conducive to their flourishing according to the best available theory of well-being.

Terminology

Before beginning the discussion of liberal neutrality it is worth briefly adumbrating the relevant terminology and some core features of the relevant theories. I use the term 'liberal neutralists' to refer to any theorist who accepts the principle of neutrality, defined as the view that 'the justification for laws and policies must not rely on any contested conception of the good'. A 'conception of the good' is a set of beliefs and commitments about what human flourishing requires. The most widely discussed liberal neutralists are a group of theorists known as 'political liberals', following Rawls' characterization of this position. Political liberalism is a complex view, but the essential argument is that the state, and all principles of justice that govern state behaviour, must remain neutral because of 'the fact of reasonable pluralism'. Disagreement about ethics is the natural result of human reason under conditions of freedom, such that in any free society we should expect disagreements about morality or ethics among reasonable people. The word 'reasonable' here refers to people who are acting in good faith and who accept that others may disagree with them about ethics. This disagreement justifies neutrality because of the liberal principle of legitimacy, according to which the use of public power must be justified to all citizens in terms they can reasonably accept. I explore this principle in more depth later in the chapter, but in brief Rawls believes that citizens can reasonably reject laws premised on ethical beliefs they do not share. The result is that participants in debates on 'constitutional essentials' (or perhaps all policies, see Quong, 2004) cannot appeal to their own beliefs about what makes for a good life. Instead, political liberals believe that policies are justified according to an 'overlapping consensus' of liberal values to which citizens can all subscribe despite their ethical commitments. Some of my arguments are directed specifically at political liberals and I will make it clear when that is the case; other arguments target the wider set of liberal neutralists who offer other arguments for neutrality. The alternative to liberal neutrality is a family of theories known as 'perfectionist'. Perfectionists take the view that the role of the state is to enable people to live good lives; thus, knowing what kind of institutions should exist requires a guiding theory of what makes for a good human life.

Arguments for neutrality

Epistemic

Epistemic arguments for neutrality rest on the difficulty of knowing what constitutes a flourishing human life. In Chapter 3 I put forward a list of valuable functionings as constitutive of a flourishing life. The epistemic objector asks how I know, or can prove, that goodness consists of the items on this list. To make sense of this kind of objection, it is useful to distinguish between a strong and a weak variant:

Strong epistemic neutrality: There cannot be 'knowledge' about ethics even in principle since all ethical claims are merely statements of feelings or preferences.

Weak epistemic neutrality: There may be truths about ethical matters, but ethical knowledge cannot be held with sufficient confidence to justify perfectionist policies.

The strong epistemic argument for neutrality is a form of moral scepticism, a widely held position in meta-ethics according to which there is no such thing as a 'moral fact' and thus no 'right' answer to moral questions (Sinnott-Armstrong, 2006). Instead, moral opinions are best understood as mere preferences or tastes. This seems to provide an argument for neutrality, in so far as it leads to the conclusion that there are no good reasons for the state to pursue any ethical value over another.

There are many different varieties of moral scepticism and assessing their merits is well beyond the purview of this book, but, fortunately, such an assessment is unnecessary because ethical scepticism cannot provide a sound argument for political neutrality. Ethical scepticism not only impugns claims about what constitutes human flourishing but rules out *all* moral claims, including the positive arguments for neutrality and beliefs about what justice requires. According to liberal neutralists, *justice* requires that the state takes no stance on matters of ethics or metaphysics. Their view is thus that there are moral reasons to favour one set of policies (the neutral ones) and to disfavour others. But if such scepticism is true then there are no moral reasons of this kind. The neutralist's view, in accordance with mine, is a substantive view about what morality requires in the case of children. Defenders of neutrality must provide reasons that count against promoting controversial ideals but that do *not* undermine their own moral ideals.

The modest epistemic argument for neutrality is more promising. Ethics is undoubtedly a complex business and the views of well-informed and sensible people differ substantially. The state should be neutral because it cannot be sure which ethical views are right and which are wrong. The most prominent modest epistemic arguments draw on a concept from Rawls' *Political Liberalism*, known as 'the burdens of judgement', though I do not think Rawls is really making an epistemic argument.[1] The burdens of judgement are a collection of factors that explain the disagreement about ethics among reasonable people. They include the fact that matters of ethics are highly complex, that people's history can bias them towards some ethical opinions over others and that it is difficult to access all the relevant evidence (Rawls, 1993: 54–8). Rawls believes that while, in the long run, we should expect some consensus among relevant experts on questions of empirical fact, the burdens of judgement imply that people will persistently disagree about even the most basic elements of ethics and theology. While the burdens of judgement are a specifically political liberal idea, other epistemic arguments have also been advanced that draw on further reasons to doubt the strength of ethical knowledge. In various ways, things such as the burdens offer an argument for neutrality in something like the following form:[2]

Premise 1: The state ought not to promote a conception of the good without sufficient confidence in its soundness.

Premise 2: The burdens of judgement – or a similar idea – mean that no ideal can be held with sufficient confidence to justify its imposition on others.

While each premise of the argument is initially plausible, both must eventually be rejected. The problem with premise 1 is that there are often costs to inaction as well as to action. Premise 2 overstates the scope of the burdens of judgement (or other similar considerations); while ethics is complex there are many ideals which can be held with justified confidence.

To illustrate the problem with premise 1, consider the following case:

School choice: A bureaucrat, Martha, is deciding whether to fund a small local school, or to use the money to expand a larger school further away and send all the local children there. Most students at the local school went to nursery together and can be expected to continue their friendships and spend a lot of time in each other's company outside of school. The other school is further away but is a leading school academically and has access to a greater range of extra-curricular activities such as art or music.

While mundane, Martha's decision turns on complex issues about what would be best for the children. Keeping the local school open will facilitate stable relationships and will reduce the costs of travelling for both children and their parents. Conversely, sending the children to the larger school promotes learning and extra-curricular attainment. Making this choice therefore requires some heuristic for comparing the importance of artistic achievement against the boredom of commuting, or ease of access to friends against likely income gains from better academic results. These kinds of questions are precisely the ones to which the burdens of judgement should apply. Nevertheless, it cannot be *impossible* for Martha to make a reasoned choice (and, note, her choice in this matter would be an action of the state).

Now suppose that if Martha does nothing the result will be that both schools are shut down so all the children will end up at a school that is even further away and does not score well academically. The uncertainty between the first two options does not count as a reason against making some choice, because Martha is sure that doing *nothing* would lead a very bad outcome. In many instances we have reason to think that the costs of inaction are high and thus (absent other arguments) sometimes the state should act even when extremely uncertain about what is best because there may be good reason to think that the status quo is worse.

The problem with premise 2 is that while there are certainly some ethical issues on which it is very difficult to come to an answer, there are many others in which this is not the case. More formally, while the burdens of judgement are a plausible way of accounting for some of the ethical disagreements in society, they are a very poor explanation for some other aspects. Rather, a great deal of the controversy about the good is explained by factors including:

1. People uncritically following the views of their parents or local communities.

2. The self-interest of dominant groups in society.
3. A pernicious media environment driven by ideology and with poor fact checking.
4. Lack of public trust in figures who have access to the right information.

These factors (and many others) are sources of *unreasonable* disagreement. By this I mean a disagreement in which the views of one side are not held with sufficiently good evidence or rationale and would be rejected by all or most relevant experts. Both sources of disagreement can operate at the same time. It is entirely consistent to accept that burdens of judgement exist and explain some forms of disagreement but still to believe that much ethical disagreement in contemporary societies is unreasonable rather than reasonable in nature.

Dissecting which beliefs are epistemically reasonable and which are not is a daunting task. However, all that I need in order to show why the state should not be neutral about all ethical disputes is to claim that many children come to hold *patently* unreasonable ethical views, and that holding these unreasonable views is bad for their welfare both directly (because possessing knowledge is itself an aspect of the good life) and indirectly if it leads them to pursue aims which are less valuable than other options. The idea is that the state should at least be permitted to act against the propagation of ethically unreasonable views to children, since children's malleability makes them vulnerable to accepting things without good reason that turn out to be bad for them and for others. The theoretical implication is that the state should only be neutral on matters on which there is genuine reasonable disagreement caused by the burdens of judgement and that many other ethical views will not count as reasonable.

This seemingly modest suggestion – to limit the scope of reasonable disagreement to views that people could accept with good reasons – goes against the writings of many political liberals. Rawls writes that 'there are no restrictions or requirements on how religious or secular doctrines are to be expressed; these doctrines need not, for example, be by some standards logically correct, or open to rational appraisal, or evidentially supportable' (2001b: 592). Quong suggests that, on the political liberal view, 'we are not meant to require anything of anyone's comprehensive views, other than that they must be *compatible* with a liberal conception of political justice' (2011: 296). The set of things that counts as 'reasonable' is thus much larger than the set of beliefs which can be held with good reason. There can be no epistemic argument for neutrality about even these ethical matters, since political liberals like Quong and Rawls have conceded that some supposedly reasonable ethical doctrines are indeed patently false.

Therefore, the continuation of a large set of false empirical beliefs about the world and faulty moral beliefs is not best explained by appealing to deep facts about the limits of reason. Instead, much disagreement persists because people, and especially children, are likely to accept the beliefs of the community around them. Therefore, I can fully accept that there are good reasons for principles of justice to avoid taking a side on ethical matters which are genuinely unclear, but there is no reason to think this kind of epistemic argument can support liberal neutrality in all or even most cases. Thus far, defenders of liberal neutrality have offered no reason why justice is not furthered by working against the sources of unreasonable disagreement and creating conditions under which children are likely to come to hold a more plausible conception of the good.

Equal concern and respect

A number of prominent writers have defended liberal neutrality by appealing to what Charles Larmore terms 'a norm of equal respect' (1987: 59–60). Ronald Dworkin believes that the state owes its citizens equal concern and that this justifies neutrality because 'since the citizens of a society differ in their conceptions, the government does not treat them as equals if it prefers one conception to another' (2000: 191). Dworkin's idea is that the state cannot favour the aims of any its citizens even if they are in fact better or more worthy and, as such, a perfectionist state seems wrongfully biased in favour of some of its citizens.

However, the equal concern argument reveals the ongoing problem with theories of justice assuming that the proper subject is the adult citizen, who comes complete with an existing conception of the good. Considering only adults, it seems reasonable to say that respecting a person means respecting the beliefs they already have. But in the case of children the situation is very different. As I have repeatedly stressed throughout the book, children's interest is not in having their beliefs respected (since young children do not have beliefs of this kind), rather it is in *acquiring* a conception of the good that is right for them and does not cause them to undermine the interests of others. The result is that proper concern for a child does not provide a reason to be neutral about ethics. Instead concern for that person pushes towards ensuring that they are guided to things that are good for them rather than ways of living which will hold them back.

Therefore, the implications of equal respect provide another way in which the case of children must be thought of as central to questions of justice, not an issue that can be tagged on later. Given that everyone is a child during some part of their life, it does not make sense for anyone to say that all that respect entails is liberal neutrality. As Quong writes, 'perfectionism allows the state to treat citizens as if they were children, in need of guidance and direction about their own lives' (2011: 315). Here Quong seemingly concedes that perfectionism directed at children would be permissible, at least in so far as the duty of respect is concerned. What he misses is the sweeping importance of this, perhaps because the case of children is taken to be a somewhat side issue. Instead, our duties towards children affect not just the design of the education system, and how laws should govern parenting, but rather all our interpersonal conduct that together creates the culture in which children are raised. While it is often disrespectful to try and guide a person once they are an adult, during childhood everyone does need guidance and direction about their own lives. What form that direction should take and what balance come from the state, other citizens or parents is a large question in Part IV. Here though, I only claim that it shows a child no disrespect to design their upbringing in order to guide them towards good ways of living, and in fact we show them disrespect by thinking of them as already beholden to the choices of their parents or the community into which they are born.

Political liberal legitimacy

The final, and most significant, argument for neutrality is that only neutral laws can be properly legitimate. Legitimacy as a concept distinguishes rightful exercise of power from mere force. Often, we think about legitimacy in democratic terms, but political liberals believe that mere majoritarian democratic legitimacy is too weak, since it allows majorities to impose their will on minorities. Instead, following Rawls, they argue that a law is only properly justified if it is justified to every citizen in terms they can reasonably be expected to accept (Rawls, 1993: 136). If any citizen has a reasonable objection to a law, then this law is not properly legitimate. This principle of legitimacy provides a justification for neutrality because in a pluralistic society there are no shared ethical or metaphysical premises which can be used to justify the use of power to all citizens. For instance, a Muslim citizen cannot be expected to accept a law justified by reference to the truth of Christianity. As a result, no laws justified according to the truth of Christianity can be legitimate across a population that includes even a few Muslim citizens (or atheists or adherents of other faiths), even if the majority of the population is Christian and wants a law justified on biblical authority. The same reasoning is taken to apply to laws justified according to any views about ethics or metaphysics, since there will always be some citizens who cannot accept these ethical theories. The result is that only neutral laws and policies, supposedly acceptable to all citizens regardless of their ethical creed, can ever be legitimate.

In response, I will suggest that the political principle of legitimacy must be rejected because of what is called the asymmetry problem. The asymmetry in question is the different ways that political liberals respond to disagreements about politics as opposed to those about ethics or theology. When citizens disagree about ethical matters, political liberals argue that it would be morally wrong to favour either side. However, they respond to disagreement about politics very differently, as Rawls, Quong and many others favour redistribution of wealth and increased social spending. These economic policies are highly controversial and their aims and justification would conflict with the sincere convictions of many citizens. Just as they are characterized by deep disagreement about ethics, current liberal societies are characterized by polarization and deep disagreement about politics.[3]

The asymmetry challenge forces the neutralist to take one of two routes. They must either: (i) show why disagreements about ethics are different from disagreements about politics; or (ii) apply the principle of neutrality to both ethics and politics in a coherent and plausible way. The first strategy is pursued by Rawls himself, but most comprehensively developed by Quong, the second is explored by Gerald Gaus. I will argue that neither route is convincing.

Quong's solution to the asymmetry problem is to argue that there is an important moral difference between ethics and politics, such that only the first demands neutrality. In Quong's terminology, disagreements about ethics are always 'foundational', whereas political conflict is sometimes 'justificatory'. A foundational disagreement occurs 'when the parties do not share any premises which can serve as a mutually acceptable standard of justification' (Quong, 2011: 193), whereas a justificatory disagreement occurs when 'participants share premises that serve as a mutually acceptable standard of justification, but they nevertheless disagree about certain substantive conclusions' (Quong, 2011: 204). Quong argues that it is impermissible for one party to impose a policy based on contested beliefs when other parties foundationally disagree, but that imposition of contested ideas is permissible when the disagreement among the parties is justificatory.

Quong's distinction provides a solution to the asymmetry problem only in the case of disagreements that may occur among citizens whom he defines as reasonable. In this context, being 'reasonable' means sharing a set of basic liberal views about justice; thus such citizens' disagreements about politics will be justificatory. They all share the same basic political views, they just disagree about how best to apply them. According to

Quong, it is permissible for reasonable citizens to impose political ideas on each other, since it is allowable to impose contested ideas within justificatory disagreements. By contrast, even among reasonable persons there will still be foundational disagreements about questions of ethics. This shows that in a highly idealized society of reasonable people there is a moral difference between imposing contested political ideas as opposed to contested ethical ideas.

However, I believe that Quong's solution, while elegant, faces a dilemma. Either he will draw the category of reasonable citizens too broadly, in which case the asymmetry problem re-emerges between reasonable persons, or he will draw it too narrowly, in case we cannot consistently assume everyone will be reasonable even in an idealized well-ordered society. A broad understanding of reasonableness is suggested when Quong (2010: 233) argues that reasonable citizens need only endorse basic liberal values like freedom and equality. On this broad understanding, a citizen could be reasonable and hold a wide array of economic and political views. The problem is that contemporary societies have shown us that people can agree that freedom and equality are valuable yet continue to disagree, fundamentally, about political matters. For instance, some people believe that governments which intervene in the marketplace necessarily undermine freedom and individual rights. These people do not see the creation of welfare states as merely a slightly different interpretation of a principle they already hold. Rather, they see such states as deep threats to their core ethical beliefs, which violate important rights that for them are just as important as the social rights that institutions like universal education or health care are meant to protect. If such conservative citizens can count as reasonable then the asymmetry problem remains a live issue even in the ideal case. It is unclear how welfare states can be legitimately imposed onto them.

Alternatively, the category of reasonable citizens could be constituted so that these people are united not just by a basic commitment to freedom and equality but by a much thicker set of commitments. This is the narrow view about what being a 'reasonable citizen' means. On the narrow view, by definition, to say that a person is reasonable is to say that he or she accepts that justice requires social spending and progressive taxation. Disagreements between narrowly reasonable citizens are more similar to what might occur within a very ideologically coherent political party, and such disagreements do indeed look justificatory. However, while the narrow reading does imply that all disagreements about justice among reasonable people are foundational it creates different but equally serious problems.

For a start, the narrow reading radically redefines who counts as 'unreasonable' in ways that do not match how this term is often used or understood. For instance, Quong and other political liberals often write as if the category of unreasonable citizens is synonymous with that of dangerous extremists. We are told that 'Unreasonable doctrines are thus doctrines whose beliefs directly contradict the fundamental political values of a liberal democratic regime' (Quong, 2010: 302). Examples offered of unreasonable citizens include misogynists and members of the KKK. However, on the narrow reading, Quong is not entitled to talk about the class of the unreasonable in this way. Racists or misogynists are indeed unreasonable by this definition, but so are those who believe their religious views should have *any* political consequences or who believe that state action in the economic sphere is a threat to personal freedom. In short, a very large proportion of people in modern society will count as unreasonable on this narrow reading.

The worry is that while Quong can show why it is acceptable to impose progressive tax laws onto the set of people who already agree with them, he has not shown why such people are justified imposing their views on anyone else except to say that these others are unreasonable. But saying that someone is unreasonable does not seem like a good reason to discount their view, once it is granted that the class of unreasonable people is so large. Therefore, neither the strong nor the broad understandings of what reasonable might mean ultimately show why it is permissible to impose left liberal views of justice, but not sometimes permissible to impose views based on a contested conception of the good.

The second kind of response to asymmetry is explored by Gerald Gaus, who argues that the state cannot legitimately impose polices justified by any sectarian *political or ethical* beliefs. In his earlier work, Gaus (2003) argued that this implied that almost no actions by the state could ever be legitimate. In his more recent work, Gaus and others have explored various ways in which some kinds of social structures might be legitimate despite deep disagreement about justice (see Gaus, 2016; Vallier, 2014). In brief, Gaus believes that a relatively minimal state could be legitimate because it performs functions upon which everyone would agree. Within a minimal state people are free to band together to create social institutions, but they cannot impose these structures on everyone since some will disagree with them. There are some serious concerns as to whether Gaus' solution really is legitimate by his own lights, but the larger problem is that he makes the price of accepting the principle of political liberal legitimacy too high, especially in the context of past or current injustices.

In the economic sphere, a serious problem with Gaus' minimal state solution is that it permits previous injustices to continue to have long and significant effects. Consider the following case:

Status quo: A small group of people become wealthy via the exploitation or persecution of other groups. This wealthy elite hoard their wealth and privileges and pass them only to their own children. These children come to hold political views by which they are entitled to this wealth and status (these children are not duplicitous; they genuinely believe they are entitled to their wealth).

According to Gaus, the mere fact that these advantaged people hold the belief that they are entitled to their wealth rules out redistributive policies. The rich object to redistribution and even a democratic majority does not have the right to impose views of justice over conscientious objections. The earlier injustice thus has persisting effects because there is no legitimate way to rectify it. A similar kind of pernicious status quo can persist with respect to the ethical beliefs that children will come to hold. Mistakes about ethical matters made by previous generations have continuing effects because the mere fact that people hold mistaken beliefs is enough to block actions to combat these beliefs (even including giving children an education that allows them to critically dissect these beliefs, since some parents conscientiously object to their children receiving an advanced education).

Therefore, I believe that both potential solutions to the asymmetry problem fail, for deep rather than easily solvable reasons. The implication is that the political principle of legitimacy must be rejected. Rather, legitimacy should be understood in some other way; perhaps simply as pertaining to laws that pass a suitably democratic procedure (see Waldron 1999: 282–94 and Christiano, 1996: 35), or that legitimate laws are ones that best serve the public good. Either of these alternatives allow that sometimes perfectionist actions can be permissible and, as such, do not support liberal neutrality.

Conclusion

In this chapter I surveyed the literature on liberal neutrality, which is a necessary enquiry given this principle rules out many elements of my understanding of children's justice. I argued that none of the arguments for liberal neutrality provide good reasons to object to perfectionism, especially in the case of children. I highlighted that the principle of neutrality is at its most plausible when we consider adult subjects with well-formed beliefs and the ability to control who they interact with. In this case, a principle of letting each person get on with their own plans seems plausible and respectful. However, the case for neutrality unravelled when applied to children, as they are profoundly vulnerable to the ethical beliefs of others.

Notes

1. For a presentation of an epistemic case for political liberalism, see Peter (2013).
2. For defences of neutrality, albeit not by political liberals, see Barry (1996: 168–73) and Lloyd-Thomas (1998: 115–25).
3. For instance, see Achen and Bartels (2016) for a discussion about the importance of political polarization in the formation of tribal identities.

7

Understanding Perfectionism

In this chapter and the next, I discuss in more detail what perfectionism is and what it entails for children's upbringing. Here I show why perfectionism must mean more than the promotion of 'high culture' and cannot be understood merely in terms of the promotion of autonomy or critical reasoning. These two aims are the most discussed instances of perfectionism in the literature but give a misleading impression about what the proper goals of a perfectionist state should be. Understanding perfection as artistic achievement can be dismissed quite quickly, since no plausible view can take art or science to be the only components of human flourishing. Understanding perfection in terms of autonomy is much more compelling and grounds a plausible view about justice for children in self-development. However, while I do not deny the importance of critical thinking, I show that becoming autonomous is not enough. Instead I argue that perfectionism requires designing children's upbringing to raise the probability that they will choose to live good lives.

The relative insignificance of 'high' culture

While widely discussed, the term perfectionism is sometimes unhelpful because its meaning is ambiguous. Rawls defines perfectionism as 'directing society to arrange institutions so as to maximise the achievement of human excellence in art, science and culture'. According to this aim, 'mankind must continually strive to produce great individuals. We give value to our lives by working for the good of the highest specimens' (1999: 325). Rawls' description has two main elements: (i) that 'perfection' is about artistic intellectual 'excellence'; and (ii) that excellence is only achieved in rare cases, so that the best way to maximize perfection is by helping a few great individuals.

In policy terms, this kind of perfectionism would require significant subsidies for museums and cultural institutions or intensive courses for those children who show aptitude in arts or sciences. Some critics of perfectionism take the promotion of high culture, by funding events and institutions like the opera or art galleries, to be representative of what perfectionist policies require. However, 'perfectionism' is now used refer to *any* action by the state that rests on a contested view of ethics. For instance, Quong writes that perfectionism is the view that 'political action should be directed towards helping individuals live good lives, and discouraging individuals from living bad or worthless lives' (2011: 3). Since there are a vast number of ways the state could help people live good lives that have nothing to do with the production of 'excellence' this latter definition is very different from Rawls' original. We can thus distinguish two different formulations:

Narrow perfectionism: Politics should promote excellence by increasing the production of artistic and cultural great works.

Broad perfectionism: One reason to favour a set of political institutions is that it makes people's lives better according to the best available ethical theory.[1]

These two principles are compatible, since one potential reason to promote excellence is that it makes people's lives better. However, it is entirely possible to accept the broad perfectionist view while rejecting the narrow one, and indeed there are good reasons to do just this. The core problem with the narrow view is captured by Dworkin, who writes: 'On any plausible view of what is truly wonderful in any human life, impact hardly comes into the story at all' (2013: 198). Dworkin highlights that narrow perfectionism fails to identify most of what is 'truly wonderful' about human life. Excellent art is, of course, valuable but it is very far from the only thing that matters. A person who does nothing but work determinedly to produce 'great' art, and who lets their friendships and romantic relationships wither, should not always be thought of as someone who has lived a good life.

Further, as I argued in Chapter 4, much of the value of creativity comes from the long process of learning and development that eventually enables creation, rather than just the art or music itself. What this implies is that focusing on a few 'great' individuals, as if only they could produce value, is misguided. Rather, almost all people can realize the value of creativity to some extent, and in Chapter 5 I argued that welfare gains accruing to the worst off count more than those accruing to the advantaged. The artistic policies that follow from my version of perfectionism involve widely dispersing creative opportunities with a special focus on the disadvantaged, not lavishing resources on activities whose benefits flow to those who are already well off.

Therefore, there are decisive reasons to reject narrow perfectionism. Arts and creativity matter a great deal, and there are powerful reasons to promote them widely, but there are many other ways that the state (and, I will go on to suggest, parents) can encourage and enable children to live well.

Autonomy and 'liberal' perfectionism

By far the most significant aspect of the good discussed in contemporary liberal theory is that of personal autonomy, such that 'the valid conception of the good life for liberal perfectionists is the life of a sufficiently autonomous individual who is able to develop an authentic life plan and pursue it' (Mills, 2012: 125). For some, the promotion of autonomy is incompatible with the promotion of any other aspects of the good (Christman, 2009; Colburn, 2010). For them, the liberal state should ensure that citizens become and remain autonomous but should take no other view about what a good life looks like. As such, autonomy becomes the justification for principles of liberal neutrality like those surveyed in Chapter 6, though with the exception that the state ought to promote autonomy whereas political liberals believe promoting autonomy to be illegitimate. In contrast, liberal perfectionists like Raz and Wall do not believe that promoting autonomy is incompatible with other perfectionist actions, but do believe that autonomy should play a dominant role in perfectionist thinking. Thus, despite the great differences across the work of these authors and others, there is a large body of theorists who believe the liberal state should be in the business of promoting autonomy, and have described in great detail what autonomy is and requires, but either deliberately eschew or have paid little attention to the other aspects of the good that ought to be promoted. My claim is that the promotion of other aspects of the good should play a bigger role in thinking about justice for children and that the promotion of other aspects of flourishing can be consistent with a concern for children's autonomy.

What is autonomy?

According to the classic definition, being autonomous requires that three conditions be met. A person must have the internal capacities needed to make authentic choices, they must have an adequate set of options available and they must be sufficiently independent from others (Raz, 1988: 373). The internal prerequisites of autonomy refer principally to the skills of rational reflection and deliberation necessary to make meaningful choices. If a person does not properly understand the options available to him or her, or the likely outcomes of his or her choices, then he or she cannot make decisions in a meaningful way. It is important to note that autonomy is not just a matter of critical reflection; rather the person must have the 'self-consciousness and vigour to take control of their affairs' (Wall, 1998: 132). Being autonomous also requires having a certain kind of character, in which a person is willing to make their own decisions and stick by them rather than blindly following social conventions or the wishes of others. The second condition is that a person must have a variety of different options. It is fairly obvious that if there is only one possible way that a person can live then they cannot make their own decisions. Raz also stresses that the different options available to a person must be substantially different from one another. A person cannot just have a large range of similar ways of life open to them, but rather must have the ability to make profound choices about how they live. The independence condition requires that a person be free of the influence of others. This means they cannot be coerced into making the choices that they do. Someone faced with the choice posed by the highwayman – 'your money or your life' – does not autonomously choose to hand over his or her money. Similarly, the agent cannot be manipulated by others, such manipulation 'perverts' the way they form preferences or plans. While Raz identifies what is bad about manipulation, he is often vague on what distinguishes manipulation from permissible influence. This lack of clarity is particularly troublesome when we seek to apply the theory to children, since many aspects of upbringing might seem like manipulation in some respects. For instance, some have suggested that getting American children to say the Pledge of Allegiance is impermissible because it constitutes manipulating the child to become loyal to the state (Callan, 1999). For now, it is enough to note that manipulation provides one way to undermine autonomy and there is a wide consensus that the liberal state should be in the business of reducing the ability of some to manipulate others.

Why autonomy?

Here I survey three reasons to believe being autonomous is important for flourishing. One possibility is that autonomy has instrumental value because it raises the probability that a person finds a way of life with which they are comfortable. This argument relies on the theory of *value pluralism*, worked out by Bernard Williams (1981) among others, which holds that there are many possible ways of flourishing and that for various reasons these values cannot be combined into one life. For instance, it may be valuable to dedicate oneself wholly to a career or social movement, but also to raise a family or to travel the world. These goals stand in tension with one another and often cannot all be combined into one life. Similarly, there are many valuable features of different cultural practices, but it is impossible for one person to coherently follow all of them. Value pluralism provides a reason to value autonomy if some people flourish better in some lives as opposed to others, perhaps because their skills and aptitudes make them well suited to some lifestyles but not others. Brighouse (and others) argue that is not enough merely to live a life that is objectively valuable; rather, a person must endorse their way of life 'from the inside' (Brighouse, 2006: 17). That is, they must themselves see the value of their life or practice. For various possible reasons, Brighouse believes that some people will never be able to properly endorse some ways of living, even if such choices are genuinely good.

If these premises are true, then it would follow that autonomy has instrumental value. To understand why, suppose that there are only three ways of living in a society and that each person can only flourish in one of them. It is entirely random which people best fit each way of life. Suppose that a non-autonomous person blindly follows the way of life of their parents or community. The result is that such a person has only a one in three chance of living well. If having autonomy raises an individual's ability to both assess how well their way of life fits their character and then to revise it if there are better options available, it thereby raises the chances of them ending up in a way of life that suits them. Believing autonomy has instrumental value is entirely compatible with thinking that there are many ways of life that are non-autonomous and fully valuable (in my example, a third of non-autonomous people live fully flourishing lives), just that in general it's better to be autonomous than not.

In addition to its instrumental value, Raz argues that autonomy has special importance given the social forms that exist in Western societies and in many parts of the modern world. These social forms create conditions under which autonomous people are better able to flourish. For instance, consider different possible practices for finding a romantic partner. It might be (for the sake of argument) that having one's parents arrange a marriage has many virtues, but, given modern conditions and societal expectations, Raz believes that people who choose for themselves generally have better lives. Similar considerations apply to practices surrounding finding a career and many other aspects of life. In a sense autonomy is locally self-affirming and 'crowds out' other ways of life, such that while there are ways of living that are fully valuable and non-autonomous these are extremely difficult to pursue under modern conditions.

Finally, autonomy might have psychological importance. Julian Rotter revealed how different people have a different 'locus of control' (Rotter, 1990: 491). People with an internal locus of control believe that life events are generally caused by their own actions or behaviours, whereas those with an external locus of control believe that their life is determined either by the actions of others, by fate or by random chance. Rotter himself, along with researchers who have built on his ideas, have suggested that those with an internal view score better on many objective and subjective measures of well-being. Objectively they do better on various health outcomes (Gale, Batty and Dreary, 2008). Subjectively, they tend to be more psychologically secure and better able to cope with change (Jackson and Martin, 1998). The benefits of feeling in control of one's life constitute a more direct intrinsic reason to value autonomy.

This is only a small subset of the many reasons that autonomy might be valuable. These arguments provide a justification for a 'non-exalted' form of autonomy (Wall, 2010: 247), but they are enough to describe a set of skills and traits which make people better at taking control of some aspects of their lives and then show why, in general and under modern conditions, taking this kind of control is valuable.

What autonomy requires from the state

The protection and promotion of autonomy is an expansive goal that has implications for many aspects of society and policy. The distinctive claim of liberal perfectionists is that the just state is whatever set of institutions best enable people to live autonomous lives. For instance, rights such as freedom of movement, speech or occupation are all best understood as valuable *because* they better enable people to control their own lives. Similarly, state intervention in the economy is valuable where it is necessary to ensure that everyone has the resources in order to act autonomously and that the economy is producing enough different options about what to buy and what to do. In upbringing, the aim of fostering autonomy guides the design of the school system as well as laws structuring parenting (an issue I discuss in Part IV), so the best polices are those most likely to produce autonomous adults.

Education promotes autonomy by developing the skills and knowledge necessary to make choices. Some knowledge of the world is an important starting point. A person must be aware of some basic features of their society in order to know what options are available to them. More generally, Razian autonomy requires a kind of self-reflection that can be developed by education and schooling. Many scholars who take this approach suggest that the development of critical debate and reflection is the central purpose of schooling (see Hitchcock, 2017 and McPeck, 1981). On this approach, the best schools and curricula are not ones which merely pass on facts. Rather, education is about creating an environment in which children learn how to scrutinize arguments and evidence and how to discover new information themselves.

Another way education links to autonomy concerns the availability of options for children. A concern for autonomy might press us towards developing education that is child led, at least to some degree. Letting children decide for themselves what subjects and issues to cover in class develops skills relevant to later choices and is itself a meaningful exercise in autonomy. Later in life, education confers more options on children by giving them skills and accreditation that open career paths. More controversially, some believe that autonomy requires that students become aware of what Bruce Ackerman calls 'the great sphere' (1980: 159). What he means is that they come to see that the cultural and religious traditions of which they are a part are just small pieces within the totality of human culture. The implication is that students must be exposed to a variety of ways of life that are different from those practised by their parents and in their home community. This aim is a feature of many leading liberal discussions of education. Harry Brighouse proposes that schools bring in outside speakers who are themselves committed to different cultural and religious practices. His reasoning is that dry, abstract discussions by teachers will not present different ways of life as real options (2006: 17–20). Brighouse's concern is echoed by Eamonn Callan, who writes that children must have 'experience of entering imaginatively into ways of life that are strange, even repugnant' (1997: 152).

There has been considerable debate in the literature concerning the potential that an autonomy-promoting education might conflict with more 'traditional' ways of living which may be inhospitable for autonomy. For instance, a way of life in which a person's role in society is determined by the needs of the group or where it is considered virtuous to be strongly guided by authority figures when considering moral questions. Raz himself suggests that while there are grounds to hope that all children become autonomous, this should not come at the cost of destroying valuable ways of life and that instead the liberal state should hope for gradual change. As I explore in more detail in Part IV, liberals have argued that while parents do have a right to pass on their religious or ethical beliefs to their children, these rights come with the proviso that they raise their children to be autonomous. The implication of this position for education provision is that parents do not have legitimate grounds to object to schooling that promotes their child's autonomy up to the requisite threshold.

For this reason, liberal perfectionism is sometimes seen as hostile to some claims of religious parents when those parents are assumed to want to control the future religious beliefs of their child and thereby restrict their autonomy. However, other theorists have suggested that the promotion of autonomy need not be inhospitable to (most) forms of religious education. Burtt (2003) has argued that religious instruction, and cultural membership more generally, buttresses a stable sense of identity of a kind that is required for autonomy (in so doing she extends various arguments made by Raz himself about the importance of group membership and identity for accessing the goods of autonomy). Schouten and Brighouse both stress that autonomy is not just about ensuring that religious citizens have the capability to revise, and potentially reject, the views of their parents and community. Rather, justice requires that children who grow up in a secular context have a genuine opportunity to opt for a religious lifestyle and that those growing up in a dominant culture can affirm ways of life out of the mainstream (Brighouse, 2006: 13–20; Schouten, 2018: 1080).

The limits of autonomy

Thus far I have discussed what autonomy is and its implications for upbringing. Now I turn to the question of why the promotion of autonomy might crowd out the promotion of other aspects of well-being. A crude version of the case made by Colburn and Christman is that autonomy is about self-rule, and as such the autonomous person must be left free to decide for themselves what is valuable without an external actor trying to push them towards one alternative or another. For instance, suppose a state decides that high culture is extremely valuable, but that most sports and TV shows are empty and worthless. Seeing itself tasked with promoting its citizens' welfare, this state tries to encourage people to go to the good pursuits by subsidizing them and prevent people going to the empty pursuits by heavily taxing them. The problem is that even if some pursuits are better than others the state is directly choosing for its citizens. It, rather than they, decides what is good and what is worth pursuing. For this reason, if autonomy is extremely valuable then this kind of state interference is counterproductive. It might improve citizens' lives in some respects, but it removes an even more important element of their well-being. As such, perfectionist theories that go beyond promoting autonomy are self-defeating.

This tension between autonomy and an interventionist state is increased due to the importance of personal endorsement. Will Kymlicka writes: 'no life goes better by being led from the outside according to values the person doesn't endorse. My life only goes better if I'm leading it from the inside, according to my beliefs about value' (1989: 12). The importance of endorsement shows a further reason why state actions to promote good living will often fail. Suppose the state acts to ensure that most citizens go to the opera, which I have stipulated to be valuable, but that most people do not want to go nor see the artistic merits of opera. Even supposing that their aesthetic judgement is mistaken, the bare fact that they do not endorse the activity takes away much of its value *for them* and thus shows another way in which perfectionism might be counterproductive.

At the extreme, as per Colburn's view, these kinds of arguments show that no kind of perfectionism is permissible because of the importance of personal autonomy. However, liberal perfectionists like Raz and Wall deny that autonomy rules out the promotion of other goods. For them, as I discussed, what matters is merely that a person is not subject to unwarranted coercion and manipulation and that they have a good range of options from which to choose. They argue that taxation and subsidy need not constitute coercion. Rather, they are simply ways the state determines the economic rules of the game to fulfil its proper (perfectionist) aims. As such, it would be entirely permissible for the state to tax unworthy pursuits in order to subsidize better ones, so long as there was a sufficiently wide range of options for people to choose from. I believe that Raz and others make their case more successfully than their interlocutors and that a person's interest in agency is met so long as they have access to good options and no outside actor is trying to predetermine how they will live their lives. Nevertheless, even according to Raz and Wall, the liberal state is highly constrained in its actions by the need to preserve the autonomy of citizens.

Autonomy and perfectionism in childhood

Earlier in this chapter I discussed three reasons the perfectionist state should concentrate only on autonomy. Going beyond autonomy is usually overly *coercive*, it is *unnecessary* because an autonomous person can find their own way to flourish and it is *self-defeating*. Here I show that none of these reasons apply in the case of children, and thus a perfectionist state should aim to more directly encourage children to live well.

The general concern about paternalistic or coercive interventions can be dismissed because it is widely accepted that direct interventions in children's lives are permissible. Children's intense vulnerability often means that coercing them for their own good – paternalism – is appropriate in a way that would not be the case for adults. The very word *paternalism* implies wrongfully treating someone as a child, yet one cannot wrongfully treat a child as a child. To give one obvious example, it is permissible to require at least young children, and possibly people as old as 18, to go to school, whereas mandatory laws requiring adults to go to school would be paternalistic and would be wrong even if the adults in question would benefit. The moral permissibility of using some kinds of coercion against children means that many more direct ways of intervening in their lives are permissible, and hence the scope to promote goods other than autonomy is significantly increased.

Perfectionism aimed at children can also dodge the worry of being self-defeating. Perfectionism for children is not chiefly about changing the incentives of those with reasonably stable sets of goals and plans; rather, it is about shifting the environment in which they form those goals. The hope is that exposing children to valuable activities, and giving them the skills and time to participate in these projects, will cause them to develop an appreciation for the value in question. If successful, this would include meaning that the child *endorses* this way of living.

Finally, and most importantly, becoming autonomous is not enough to ensure that children will flourish. As such, seeing a perfectionist state as only about promoting autonomy is insufficient to meet children's interests. While it is vitally important that people are able to take control of their own lives, to exit a practice or relationship when it no longer works for them, it is simply unreasonable to think that the choices we make will not be explained in large part by the conditions of our upbringing and social circumstances.

For many people, their childhood has a lifelong effect on their values and practices: the implication is that while autonomy may have great instrumental value, it does not suffice to protect children's interest. If people could easily shift their commitments and change their patterns of living then there would be no reason to worry about them being socialized into practices or beliefs which are empty or harmful. However, this assumption requires a form of autonomy well beyond that which can plausibly be assumed as part of a theory of children's justice. After all, our experience of life in diverse societies suggests that people's ethical commitments are often highly resistant to change and that many beliefs and practices adults learn as children are very persistent. For instance, large proportions of people stick with the religious faith of their parents or with their parents' political affiliations (Achen and Bartels, 2016: 233). This occurs even in societies where people have access to high-quality education, often to degree level. I do not suggest that such effects are necessarily problematic, but they do imply that upbringing is likely to have an important effect on a person's later beliefs, even when the individual is 'autonomous' according to all but the most implausibly demanding standard. This in turn suggests that we do have reason to care about the content of the ways of life into which children are socialized. In a just society we should care that people generally grow up in patterns of living that are good for them, since they will often be tied to such ways of living even if they later learn to think critically. Working out what kinds of patterns of living can be judged good for children is the task of Chapter 8.

Conclusion

In this chapter, I focused on what it means for a theory to be perfectionist. I discussed the relatively low importance of great artistic or intellectual achievements and instead suggested that while the protection of creativity was important its value can be realized by almost all people. I then looked at liberal perfectionism and the aim of promoting autonomy. I illustrated why autonomy is valuable for instrumental reasons: because people are more likely to end up in a life that works for them and because there is intrinsic value in having control over one's life. Realizing this value means that children must come to have skills of critical reasoning, an awareness of the various options in their society and the emotional resources to change their life if they so choose. This might conflict with the wishes of their parents, though the depth of this conflict can be overstated. However, I then showed that because children's interest in autonomy is much weaker, there is much more scope for the state and other actors to improve their lives more directly. Since everyone is a child for some of their lives the implication is that there is much more scope for the direct promotion of contested, but valuable, ways of living.

Note

[1] This usage of narrow and broad is different to that of Hurka's, whose view can be characterized as a particularly well-developed 'broad' perfectionism according to my terminology (Hurka, 1993: 4).

8

The Implications
of Perfectionism

Children's justice requires promoting not merely autonomy but, more directly, encouraging children's core interests. This entails a working theory of what those interests are, as raised in Chapter 3. There I introduced Nussbaum's list of capabilities as a placeholder for the kinds of goods that together constitute flourishing. While I commended this list as a basis for discussion, I suggested a potential problem in so far as Nussbaum and Sen believed that the list of goods should be neutral between all competing conceptions of the good. In light of the arguments of the previous chapters, we can see there is no good reason to accept this neutrality restriction. In this chapter I thus develop a list freed from this constraint. I then explore what kinds of ethical views might best promote interests understood in this way.

An objective list of well-being

In order to meet the aim of neutrality, both Sen and Nussbaum discuss well-being in highly general terms. There are some good grounds to think that even Nussbaum's list fails to achieve this aim of neutrality and that some people might not be able to accept some of the items on the list (see Nelson, 2008: 99). More fundamentally, the problem with a neutral list is that it cannot serve a properly critical function. Often, we need more detail on what instances of a thing count as valuable goods and which do not, but making such judgements requires wading into ethical controversy. For instance, Nussbaum believes that sexual intimacy is one important source of flourishing, contributing to a special kind of affiliation with others. On the face of it, this claim is very general and compatible with almost all conceptions of the good. However, knowing what people's interests consist of requires knowing not only that sexual intimacy can be valuable, but what instances of it have value. This second issue is deeply controversial; some people think that all instances of pleasurable sex have value and perhaps that sex with different partners makes things more exciting, but others consider that the value of sex depends on being in a long-term relationship. Some believe that only heterosexual sex is valuable, but many others deny this. In short, to have a grasp on whether a child's life is currently going well, or is likely to go well in the future, it is often necessary to make controversial claims about what a good life requires.

In place of an vague neutral list, I suggest an 'objective list' theory of well-being. Items are not on the list because everyone agrees to them, but rather because there is good reason to think they are objectively good things for a human life.[1] I therefore suggest that in addition to unproblematic basics like shelter and health, the following list can serve as a guide to the objectively valuable components of children's well-being. The list is, of course, very far from exhaustive, but I will show how the protection of these important goods, particularly to the worst off, requires that they and others hold certain ethical convictions.

1. **Egalitarian relationships with others**: The ability to participate with others on equal terms in the political sphere. Long-lasting personal relationships based on mutual respect and a recognition of all parties' equal status.
2. **Knowledge**: An accurate understanding of important features of the world and one's place in it.
3. **Agency**: The ability to act independently. To possess the cognitive and emotional resources to make one's own decisions across important domains of life and for one's life to be shaped by these decisions rather than those of others.
4. **Nature**: Interaction with the natural world and other species.
5. **Creativity**: An ability to create new objects and to develop skills and talents that allow for more intricate or complex forms of creation.
6. **Sexual intimacy**: With other consenting adults, of any sex or gender.

My approach replaces somewhat vague categories like 'emotions' or 'association' with more specified detail of what a valuable emotion or association would look like. Showing how this list leads to controversial, but I believe attractive, conclusions about justice requires going beyond the abstract, and thus in the rest of the chapter I discuss four different features of a good society that flow from this theory of well-being. In each case widespread acceptance of these values will promote the interests of children, particularly the worst off among them.

Social norms and sexual choice

The first example of what perfectionism for children requires is that people grow up believing in a considerable sphere of sexual freedom and that there are a range of entirely permissible sexual choices beyond the two-person heterosexual couple, including homosexuality, bisexuality and polyamory. In a just society, children will not only believe that sexual freedom is a political right, but also that sexual freedom is a permissible and potentially valuable option for them and for people they encounter. They will not refrain, for instance, from exploring possible relationships because they think they are wrong or sinful, and they will accept relationship choices made by friends and colleagues so long as they are consensual and free from objectionable forms of inequality.

While the fact that people have a political right to sexual choice is widely accepted by liberal writers, liberal neutrality requires that justice be neutral between competing conceptions of ethics, including different views about the permissibility of non-heterosexual lifestyles. The dominant position in the literature is thus that while gays and lesbians must have equal rights in the political sphere, the just society might contain many citizens who believe that some consensual sex is wrong or sinful. In Rawls' discussion of neutrality, and the ideal of public reason, he argues that in a liberal society people cannot appeal to their contested moral ideals when designing public institutions. One example is that they cannot appeal to their view that homosexuality is wrong when opposing gay marriage. This allows that the belief that homosexuality is wrong can form part of one of the views about the good that people might have in a just liberal society, but in a just society they must not appeal to this value when making policy on things like family law (Rawls, 1997: 779).

There are thus roughly two positions on what justice requires in this instance:

Acceptance: A citizen who believes non-heteronormative relationships are just as much a source of value as are heterosexual ones.

Toleration: The belief that all citizens have equal political rights, implying that it is wrong to use the power of the state to force people to adopt heterosexual relationships or to refrain from non-heterosexual ones.

While a widespread attitude of toleration would undoubtedly be an improvement on the current situation in many liberal states, my question is what a more fully just society would look like. Creating a culture in which most citizens merely tolerate homosexuality might be enough to protect the interests of adult citizens, but would, I suggest, fail to protect the vital interests of children. In this case, children's current and future well-being are threatened in three main ways by the ethical views of others: (i) they come to hold mistaken beliefs about sexual morality, which informs their views on which options are permissible for them; (ii) their parents' ethical views might undermine a relationship which is highly important for the child; and (iii) children who are homosexual are less accepted by the community they grow up in. While adults can also be harmed in similar ways, children's malleability, their dependence on their parents and their inability to control their own lives – in this case their place of residence – makes them significantly more vulnerable.

Taking the first point, in Chapter 3 I argued that children could be wronged by their upbringing if it causes them to form ethical views which hold back their flourishing. A concrete example of this is a gay person who comes to believe that homosexual sex or relationships are morally wrong or sinful. In many instances, this person will come to hold these ethical beliefs because of the influence of their parents or their community. The costs to the person of this upbringing might be extremely high. They may, for instance, deny themselves potential romantic relationships that could have been a huge source of flourishing. Research suggests that some children in communities in which anti-gay attitudes are prevalent are likely to suffer extreme emotional turmoil (Sadusky, 2018). Later in life, some such people choose a life of celibacy as a way of reconciling their faith with their sexual desires. While it is wrong to suggest that celibacy is an inherently bad choice for some people, seeing celibacy as one's only permissible option is deeply problematic (Sadusky, 2018). There is evidence that celibacy corresponds with higher rates of problematic loneliness among some gay people. Thus, in some instances children's interests (in egalitarian relationships and in emotional health) are directly imperilled by the content of their own ethical beliefs, the fact they wrongly believe an option is morally wrong when it is permissible.

With regard to the second point, mere toleration from a child's parents might often be insufficient for the child to fully realize the goods of the parent–child relationship. This occurs when parents make the relationship in some sense conditional on the child conforming to the parent's own beliefs and foregoing an LGBT (lesbian, gay, bisexual and transgender) lifestyle. Alternatively, a parent's ethical beliefs might discourage the child from coming out to their parent(s) and thus losing a potential source of support during a difficult time. There is evidence that older children in some communities often fail to disclose their sexual preferences to their parents (Savin-Williams and Vrangalova, 2013) and rely more on peers for support (Munoz-Plaza, Quinn and Rounds, 2002). Children's perceived inability to rely on their parents or wider family is problematic, since support from family is seen as an important predictor of their ability to deal with the potential emotional difficulties of coming out (Sheets and Mohr, 2009).

One might respond to this argument by suggesting that parents have a *duty* to love their children regardless of the child's sexuality (Lau, 2015). This suggestion allows theorists to criticize parents who fail to support their children without thereby taking a stand on the content of their beliefs (see Brennan and Macleod, 2017). On this view it is the parents' failure to provide adequate caring, not their homophobia itself, which matters. The potential advantage of this approach is that it is consistent with the principle of liberal neutrality. It allows liberals to criticize parental behaviours without thereby criticizing the ethical beliefs which cause those behaviours. The problem, though, is that the way parents should respond to their children depends upon the underlying morality of the case. Consider the following case:

Coming out: Ian finds out that his son Jack is gay; he is deeply hostile to LGBT lifestyles and his relationship with Jack suffers. Kyle finds out that his daughter, Laura, is seriously racist and bigoted. He deplores this new side of her character and their relationship suffers.

One possible response to this is to say that while Ian is entitled to his personal beliefs, he should put them aside when he is raising Jack to stop his ethical beliefs about homosexuality influencing their relationship. The problem is that this does not seem like the right reaction in the case of Kyle. This is because Laura has done something which is wrong and it is therefore morally appropriate for Kyle to show his disapproval. What is so appalling for Jack is that his life is being undermined because of his own *permissible* desires and choices. Only by taking a stand on the ethics of sexual choice can we capture this injustice. Thinking through the impact of homophobic parents thus shows why a theory of justice should not aim to be neutral on matters of ethics, but should instead be able to capture the profound effect that parents' ethical beliefs might have for their children.

Finally, looking at the third point, children are at risk of ethical costs because they often have little ability to control where they live and are thereby especially vulnerable to the views of those around them. Despite recent social progress, there are still many parts of contemporary liberal societies that are hostile to LGBT lifestyles. For instance, indicative studies show that around a third to half of all Americans would agree with the statement that homosexuality is 'sinful'.[2] This view is geographically concentrated, implying that there are some areas in which most people take this view. Growing up as gay in these areas means living in a place in which a core feature of one's identity is distrusted. This has provable pernicious effects on mental health; rates of depression and anxiety were found to be significantly higher among gay individuals than among heterosexual people, in extremis leading to higher rates of self-harm and suicide (see Van Bergen et al, 2013). Even absent these very severe effects, the antipathy of others in the community can have pervasive and negative effects. Aveline provides a useful example of a family who stopped receiving Christmas cards from many of their friends and neighbours once it was revealed that their son was gay (Aveline, 2004). This example is instructive in the present discussion because none of these other people was in breach of their duties to the family in question. No one is under an obligation to send Christmas cards. Therefore, this kind of treatment could persist even in a culture that tolerated homosexuality. Recall that the distinction between toleration and acceptance was that the tolerant person merely respected political equality.

While sending Christmas cards does not seem particularly important, the overall effect of lots of small acts like this is to isolate the family from their community. While we are not given any further information about the child in question, it seems reasonable to speculate that their isolation from their community placed a strain on them and that this was particularly burdensome given that they (albeit unintentionally) were the cause.

Controversial science

Children's interest in knowledge provides a useful way of distinguishing my approach from that of liberal neutralists. My view suggests that children have a direct interest in knowing what is best justified or most likely to be true and that the value to them of knowledge should inform curriculum design. In contrast, liberal neutralists believe that the state, including the education system, must be neutral on the truth or falsity of different comprehensive doctrines. This includes comprehensive doctrines that are at odds with the best available scientific or historical evidence.

Before revealing the differences between my perfectionist approach and that of neutralists it is worth noting that not all knowledge contributes to well-being. A person clearly does not have an interest in knowing (because they counted) all the blades of grass in a field. Further, all plausible theories accept that there are some forms of knowledge that have instrumental importance. For instance, people have an interest in knowing which side of the road one should drive on. Here I explore the claim that some instances of knowledge have special *intrinsic* value: for instance to know the true history of human civilizations (including the serious wrongs committed by colonial powers) and scientific theories such as evolution or the big bang. The intrinsic value of these important facts comes in understanding one's place in the world and its real nature.

A principle that requires teaching children these intrinsically important facts is highly controversial. Most obviously there is a long-standing campaign to prohibit the teaching of the theory of evolution in public schools and instead support teaching either creationism or what is known as intelligent design (ID). Creationism refers to the belief that God directly created human life in its current form and perhaps that the story of Genesis is literally true (such that He did it in only seven days). ID is a modern theory that officially holds only that evolution cannot explain all the development of life and the best explanation involves another actor directly intervening in the process. Exploring the limits of parental rights is the topic of Part IV, but for now it's enough to show why a perfectionist theory captures the best reasons we have for schools to teach children about things like evolution.

Some neutralists have argued that the state must either allow parents to teach their children whatever view of creation they favour (Vallier, 2014: 244) or must teach both ID and evolution in order to remain neutral on the question (Nagel, 1970: 188–90). In both cases the reason is that they believe that the state cannot take a view on how life was created and therefore the right policy is to leave it up to parents to try and teach a variety of options. Nagel and Vallier's view on this matter does not reflect the majority opinion of liberal neutralists. Most who have written on this issue do favour teaching evolution. However, their reasons are, for instance, the democratic importance of science (Gutmann, 1999: 102) or a concern about using public schools for sectarian purposes (Gutmann, 1999; Forrest, 2011). While both these considerations are valid, they are rather narrow in scope and do not capture the most significant reasons to care about the teaching of science. While some understanding of science is indeed very important for democratic debate, it is very rare that important matters of public concern deal directly with things like the evolution of life. It is therefore not true that a person is unable to participate as a democratic citizen if they believe in something like creationism. Similarly, if the only way we can ensure children are taught good science is in state-run schools then this aim can be subverted, as it often is in practice, by children being taken out of these schools. Therefore, on the neutralist view there are at most contingent and weak reasons to teach children about things like evolution. By contrast, on the perfectionist view we can appeal directly to the interests of children in acquiring knowledge about their world and history.

Cases such as ID also expose some of the limitations of seeing the aims of education only in terms of developing critical thinking. This idea has led some to favour 'teaching the controversy', that is, having science teachers lay out both sides of the debate (Gardner, 1984). The problem with this proposal is that children, or indeed most adults, do not have the requisite skills to meaningfully assess complex evidence. The result is that either the science teacher will themselves have to explain all the grave problems with the case for ID, which is just the same as teaching evolution, or the children will receive a presentation of false ideas which is wrongly compelling and likely to mislead. Therefore, while critical thinking is an important goal, it does not make sense to simply present all the possible theories and expect critically thinking children to select from them. Rather, it sometimes makes sense for teachers and other officers of the state to select among the available theories and to teach some as being better than others.

Therefore, one advantage of the perfectionist view of upbringing is that in some controversial cases it can offer a compelling explanation of the function of schools. On my view it is a good thing in itself that children come to know important features of their world. I believe that this kind of reasoning echoes the beliefs of many science or history teachers, who recognize the intrinsic value of these subjects rather than merely seeing their value in developing economically useful skills or facilitating democratic discussion. The intrinsic value of knowledge applies to many other subjects. A perfectionist state will teach literature or creative arts because of their intrinsic importance and direct contribution to well-being. It can thus provide a more robust reason to defend the teaching of those subjects, particularly given there may be other ways to develop the skills needed for children to participate in the economy or democratic process. In sum, I have shown that acknowledging intrinsic value is both practically important and intuitively appealing and that only a perfectionist view can properly account for this importance.

Consumerism/deep green ethos

An emphasis on material consumption is one of the definitive aspects of contemporary liberal societies and this feature of our culture is reproduced among children. Children are exposed to consumerism from a very young age, most directly from advertising. In its most extreme form advertising persuades children 'you are what you own' (Kasser, 2002: 91). Around 34 per cent of 9 to 13-year-olds say they'd rather spend time buying things than almost anything else and 45 per cent say 'the only kind of job I want when I grow up is one that gives me lots of money' (Layard and Dunn, 2009: 50). Layard and Dunn cite the work of Juliet Schor (2004), who, they suggest, demonstrates that 'the more a child is exposed to the media (television and the internet), the more materialistic she becomes; the worse she relates to her parents and the worse her mental health' (Layard and Dunn, 2009: 59).

The concern raised by these social scientists is that living in a consumerist society causes children to acquire a value set that is bad for them in major respects. In terms of a theory of justice, recognizing the importance of this research requires an evaluative theory that tracks children's well-being, rather than merely their later access to resources. What work on materialism shows us is that a focus simply on ensuring that children receive enough money might miss important other ways that the economy and culture could affect their future lives.

Also, returning to the issues discussed in Chapter 3, the metric we use to trace children's interests is relevant to evaluating the effects of consumerism on children. For instance, there is an ongoing controversy in economics and psychology about the extent to which raising incomes boosts a person's happiness. Famously, research by Richard Easterlin suggested that while within a country more income boosted happiness, between countries there was no correlation between income and happiness and rising incomes over time do not contribute to increased happiness (Easterlin, 1974).[3] However, this debate sometimes assumes a hedonistic view in which happiness corresponds with flourishing and thus the question is merely whether higher consumption raises reported life satisfaction. On my view, while positive emotions are important, what really matters is whether rising incomes correspond with things that are intrinsically valuable and contribute to well-being. What matters is the effects of consumerism on significant goods like interpersonal relationships, our ability to utilize our talents and access to the natural world.

Seen in this light, there is powerful evidence to suggest that consumerism has negative effects on well-being. Psychological studies have suggested that people who prioritize material success often do so at the expense of their close friendships and romantic relationships (for instance, see Richins and Dawson, 1992: 20–1 and Schmuck, Kasser and Ryan, 2000). Kasser summarizes the evidence as follows: 'materialistic values lead people to "invest" less in their relationships and their communities. Notably, this relative lack of care for connectedness is reflected in low-quality relationships characterised by little empathy and generosity, and by objectification, conflict and feelings of alienation' (2002: 72). Feelings of objectification and alienation are ways in which consumerism undermines not merely emotions and mental states, but the objective bases of human flourishing.

In addition to damaging personal relationships, materialism also carries heavy environmental costs. As is now widely known, anthropogenic climate change is highly likely to cause severe damage to food production, to increase the risk of flooding and to cause disruptive weather patterns (Wallace-Wells, 2019). The causes of these problems are complex, but they are at least in part caused by rising consumption and by the kinds of consumption in which society engages. Neutrality-based views of justice are not well placed to capture all of the costs of environmental damage. While they can adequately show the importance of protecting the environment for some instrumental reasons, they miss other more direct ways in which damage to the natural world causes the loss of value both to humans and other species. The reason is that the intrinsic value of nature is a contested ethical value and, as such, not something which liberal neutralists believe should justify policies. Thus, a state governed on neutral principles cannot appeal to the intrinsic value of nature, or the natural world's direct contribution to well-being, when justifying which institutions should govern children's lives.

For instance, liberal, neutralist Brian Barry believes that while he himself is convinced of the need to protect the environment, this kind of 'eco centrism' is just another contested moral view that cannot form the basis of public policy (Barry, 1996: 171). Similarly, while Elizabeth Cripps (2017a, 2017b) recognizes that parents have a special responsibility to raise environmentally conscious children, she argues that it is wrong to try and promote a 'deep green' comprehensive conception of the good. A deep green ethos is defined as one assigning intrinsic moral significance to the survival of non-humans or ecosystems (Cripps, 2017b: 42), which she suggests must be rejected because of the importance of liberal neutrality (Cripps, 2017b: 53).

In contrast, according to my account, justice should be sensitive to the loss of well-being, and of intrinsic goods, that occur due to environmental degradation. I believe that views which deny the political relevance of this value are impoverished. To illustrate this difference, consider the following case:

Environmental choice: The industrial activity of a society is causing environmental damage to a river that many people live close to. This causes the river to flood more regularly, damaging the livelihoods of those within a poor community who live nearby and a series of forests that are habitats for different species. The society has three options: (i) it can leave the people near the river; (ii) it can move the people into similarly good housing that will never flood; or (iii) it can repair the damage so the river does not flood.

Suppose that repairing the damage is the costliest option and that leaving the people near the river is the cheapest. There are neutral reasons of justice to favour protecting the worst-off people living near the river and therefore choosing the second option over the first. However, there are no such reasons to favour the second over the third option and there are public reasons of cost to prefer the second. Thus, this society is permitted and perhaps even required by justice to destroy the forest. Further, on some views, citizens who value nature could not refer to this value when determining what to do (see Quong, 2004). The problem is that the calculus has missed one huge consideration, namely the importance that interactions with nature and animal life has for people, especially future generations.

In various ways then a consumerist culture can damage the interests of children. This example thus provides a good illustration of two key aspects of my view. First, that justice must be concerned with the effects of institutions and culture on well-being, not merely resources, so that it can appropriately measure the damage caused by, for instance, stress engendered by consumerism. Secondly, justice cannot be neutral about some ethical controversies. While some people believe that nature and animal life is unimportant, I have argued it forms part of children's interests to access these goods and that this provides a reason for the destruction of nature to count as unjust.

Gender norms

Finally, I argue that justice requires the creation of egalitarian family structures. By egalitarian, I mean that there are no assigned roles because of gender (though there may be many permissible reasons to assign people different roles in the home). There are many reasons to think that such families are required by justice, but I focus on the impact on the next generation. Specifically, the aim is that girls come to have similar aspirations to boys and neither group sees their future role as set by their gender.

While there are ongoing questions about whether there are any 'natural' differences between the biological sexes, it seems unarguable that at least a good deal of gender inequality is driven by cultural norms and practices. Gendered norms harm girls' interests by making it more likely that they will lack the resources and chances for pursuing some competitive careers and projects. Arlie Hochschild described women working 'the second shift' in the home, work comparable to another part-time job in addition to their paid commitments (Hochschild, 1989). Recent research from the ONS (2016) in the UK has found that even when paid work commitments are equal, women do five to seven hours' more work than men.[4] Beyond their economic impacts, gendered norms undermine women's interests in agency and in equal relationships with others.

My position on this issue contrasts with the view of liberal theorists like Rawls who argued that even idealized principles of justice cannot demand an equal division of labour. The reason is that requiring the equal division of household labour conflicts with liberal freedoms of association and choice. He believes if a woman chooses to do more than her fair share then this must be permissible. Rawls writes:

> One cannot propose that equal division of labour in the family be simply mandated, or its absence in some way penalized at law for those who do not adopt it. This is ruled out because the division of labour in question is connected with basic liberties, including the freedom of religion ... It is only involuntary division of labor that is to be reduced to zero. (2001a: 162)

Rawls draws attention to women who choose to do more domestic labour for cultural or religious reasons, and he thereby connects the debate on gender norms to questions of cultural freedom and on multiculturalism.[5] This is somewhat regrettable, since it might seem to imply that unequal gender norms are a feature only of non-Western cultures, whereas, of course, Western societies are riven by deep and persistent gender inequalities. Nevertheless, the debate on this set of issues provides useful insight into why making the case of children central to debates about justice and gender is vital.

To illustrate, consider the views of Susan Moller Okin, who believed that liberal multiculturalism was 'bad for women' because many cultural practices are fundamentally gendered. Okin argues that the problem with multiculturalism is that it permits the continuation of these gendered groups and thereby sacrifices the interests of the girls in those groups. She writes that 'group rights are potentially, and in many senses actually, antifeminist. They substantially limit the capacities of women and girls of that culture to live with human dignity equal to that of men and boys, and to live as freely chosen lives as they can' (Okin, 1993: 12).

Okin's point is that the choices of any one woman cannot be taken in isolation and that justice must consider the collective result of choices that create social pressure on others. Okin's argument is at its most salient when we consider the effects of cultural norms on children. Children's views on gender norms are highly influenced by the way those norms are displayed by their parents and wider society (e.g. see Edlund and Oun, 2016). How people choose to act in their own home affects their children and, through later peer group effects, impacts the balance of views held in the rest of society.

The potentially serious costs of Rawls' view are demonstrated by his belief that liberalism must be comfortable with religious minorities who want to live apart from society. Rawls distinguishes his political liberalism from alternative views by arguing that it

> will ask that children's education include such things as knowledge of their constitutional and civic rights so that, for example, they know that liberty of conscience exists in their society and apostasy is not a legal crime, all this to insure that their continued membership when they come of age is not based simply on ignorance of their basic rights or fear of punishment for offences that do not exist. (1993: 199)

Given the context, it seems reasonably clear that Rawls is referring to groups like the Amish, following the US Supreme Court case of Wisconsin vs Yoder, in which an Amish family tried to remove their children from education at age 14 (1972). One relevant feature of Amish life is their sharply gendered social norms. The fact that Rawls believes such groups should be able to continue such practices even in a just society is evidence for Okin's charge that Rawls is insufficiently attentive to the interests of young women. In this instance, while they are not *legally* forced to remain in gendered circumstances, they nevertheless face significant, perhaps overwhelming, social pressure to do so. While groups like the Amish are more sharply gendered than is the norm, problematic norms persist across many parts of modern societies. A theory comfortable even with the extreme cases seems to entail that widespread gendered norms persist in more mundane cases.

In response to these kinds of concerns, some political liberals have put forward the idea that Rawls' framework is more hospitable to feminist concerns than some of his own remarks on this subject suggest (see Neufeld 2009; Schouten, 2017). Significantly, these arguments often draw on the importance of role models for children. For instance, Schouten has argued that political liberalism is compatible with, and in fact requires, robust actions to secure gender equality because of the importance of role models for children. The idea is that while society should be neutral about family choice, gender norms become problematic when they constrain the real choice of future generations (Schouten, 2017: 183).

That theorists turn to the impact of gender norms on future generations highlights the fundamental importance of childhood to liberal theorizing. Absent the circumstances of childhood, it is much more plausible to think that gendered patterns of living are consistent with justice. After all, each woman has a right to choose to live in a gendered fashion if she so desires.

It would be consistent with justice for many people to choose gendered patterns of living, but because of children's vulnerability to social pressure that kind of gendered society becomes unjust.

As a matter of exegesis, I think Rawls himself would reject that political liberalism would require egalitarian family norms, even when accounting for the impact of gender norms on children. If political liberalism does require egalitarian families, then there is little to divide political liberalism from perfectionist or comprehensive liberal accounts of family ethics. But Rawls explicitly suggests that political liberalism requires 'far less' than would be required by other kinds of liberal theory and cites this difference as the core advantage of his view (1993: 199). At least in Rawls' mind then, the attraction of political liberalism in this case is that it permits a much wider variety of family forms, including those with a deeply gendered structure. In this context it is notable that other political liberals agree with Rawls' initial remarks and see it as attractive that political liberalism can 'accommodate a wide variety of different family forms, from feminist to traditional illiberal conceptions' (De Wijze, 2000: 280).

Thus, while I entirely concur with those feminists who argue that families should be egalitarian because of the effects of norms on children, I believe that their view rests on an overly broad understanding of what Rawls means when he says that citizens have an interest in 'the capacity to form and revise a conception of the good'. Thus their view become almost indistinguishable from the supposedly perfectionist view that I appeal to, for example in its interest in agency or in egalitarian personal relationships. While the framing of the argument is important in some respects, this issue should not obscure the central point of agreement between my view and more feminist versions of political liberalism nor our shared disagreement with many other defenders of liberal neutrality. The central point is that while justice among adults might be consistent with chosen disadvantages that align with gender, such inequalities are rendered unjust by their effects on the next generation. Girls' and young women's interests can be greatly undermined by growing up in a gendered society and, for this reason among many others, in a just society families should be egalitarian.

Conclusion

The point of each of these cases is to highlight different ways in which imagining a fully just society for children requires taking a side in some of the fiercest ethical questions that divide modern society. Many of the most persistent ethical disagreements in contemporary society concern issues such as gender roles, sexual norms and environmentalism or consumerism. To say that justice should take a stand on these questions is simply to say that there is good reason to think that one set of ideals, socially liberal ones, are better for human flourishing than are competing ideals. These examples show what would follow for the state according to my theory. Namely that the design of social institutions should promote, as far as possible, such socially liberal views. In Part IV I show that parents also have duties to promote such patterns of living.

Notes

[1] Richard Arneson proposes a similar objective modification to Nussbaum's list, although he does not specify the items on the list as I do here (Arneson, 2010: 108).

[2] See, for instance, https://www.theatlantic.com/politics/archive/2014/09/half-of-americans-believe-gay-sex-is-a-sin/380567/.

[3] Although this research has since been seriously critiqued, for instance see Angus Deaton (2008) and Stevenson and Wolfers (2008).

[4] See Office for National Statistics, https://www.ons.gov.uk/employmentandlabourmarket/peopleinwork/earningsandworkinghours/articles/womenshouldertheresponsibilityofunpaidwork/2016-11-10.

[5] See Mookherjee (2008, 2011) for arguments that suggest multiculturalism can be reconciled with feminist concerns.

PART IV
The Rights and Duties of Parents

9

The Project View of Parenting

The role of Part IV in the ongoing argument of this book is to integrate the morality of parenting into the perfectionist view developed earlier. According to my theory, the best set of institutions are the ones that best enable people to live flourishing lives and the best set of childrearing practices are the ones that best promote children's interests, as described in previous chapters. In this chapter, I discuss how this view of politics might seem deeply hostile to parental rights and instead require that children are raised by whomever is best placed to care for them. Against this challenge, I show that the special value of parenting means that all people should have access to a secure right to become a parent.

The best available parents

Biological parents are presumed to have powerful rights to look after their own children and most children in contemporary liberal societies are raised by one or both of their biological parents. While the state has the power to remove children from their parents, such power is used only in extreme cases. However, while the practice of entrusting children to the adults who created them is well established, there is no necessary reason why society must be organized this way. Children could be allocated to whoever is most likely to care for them effectively. This is the best available parent view (BAP). While intuitively troubling – since it would require the redistribution of children – the BAP flows from the highly plausible view that parental rights are justified by appeal to the child's own interests in having their basic needs met and in qualities such as special attachment and love (see Lau, 2015).

This view of parental rights is known as a fiduciary approach, since parents only acquire rights because the child requires them to have such powers. It follows that the question of who has parental rights should be determined by the child's needs. This way of thinking mirrors other cases in which someone gains rights over another person who is incapacitated, such as those granted powers over someone with dementia. In such cases one person makes decisions on another's behalf, but the scope and duration of these rights is determined by the interests of the cared-for party. Thus, the prospective parent's own desires and interests should not play a *justificatory* role. Peter Vallentyne argues:

> Given that the child has independent moral standing, and the rights at issue are rights to control access to the child, it is quite plausible that the child's interests take priority over the potential custodial parent's interests. A man's profound interest in having a relationship with a given woman does not give him any rights to control access to her. The situation with children is no different. (2013: 1001)

To illustrate the implications of BAP, consider the following:

Baby redistribution: Neil and Olivia have a baby, Paul. Just before Paul's birth Neil leaves Olivia, escapes paying child support and is never heard from again. Olivia has a low income and she is under serious stress from her time-consuming job. Nevertheless, she will be able to provide all of Paul's basic needs. Quinn is infertile but wants to become a mother and would be excellent at this role.

According to the BAP, the state would be justified in taking Paul away from Olivia and giving custodial rights to Quinn. While this intervention would make Olivia worse off, her interests should not be relevant in assigning care over Paul because what matters is *his own* interests. Note that assigning care over Paul does not (necessarily) reflect praise for Quinn or blame for Olivia. Defenders of the BAP need not think that people who are unable to provide care for children are bad people or should be subject to sanctions. In this instance, Olivia's situation seems Neil's fault not her own. However, while she should not be blamed, her circumstances might imply that Paul is better off with someone else assigned as his parent.

Therefore, while intuitively repugnant, the BAP has a plausible justification. Showing why it fails requires either demonstrating why the fiduciary view does not imply the BAP, or why the fiduciary view is misguided. I now briefly consider then reject two ways of blocking the BAP consistent with the fiduciary view. I show that these arguments fail and the better response involves rejecting the fiduciary view and insisting that the interests of parents are directly relevant in assigning parental rights.

One way to block the BAP is to note the terrible consequences that would occur if this policy were ever enacted. Given that most biological parents deeply desire to look after the children they create there would have to be invasive police action to redistribute children to better available parents. Since many people would not want to have children unless they knew they would be the parents the birth rate would catastrophically decline. However, while these consequences are important, appealing to these bad consequences provides at most a contingent justification for parental rights. The bad consequences of BAP cannot explain why people are *justified* in their belief that they ought to be the ones to care for their child.

To illustrate, compare these two possible interventions. In the first case, a state sends in troops to evict a man from his legally acquired home so that the state can build a statue of the president. The homeowner will likely feel extreme distress and this distress goes a long way to show why the action is deeply wrong. In the second case, the police throw a squatter out of another person's house. Suppose the squatter loved living there, but had no claim to it and the real owner wanted to get back in. Perhaps the squatter would be just as upset as would the man in the first case. However, the fact that the legal owner's feelings are justified makes them much more morally relevant. Similarly, Olivia's distress at losing Paul matters not just because all distress is bad, but because it seems intuitively to be a justified response to an injustice. What is needed is a way of explaining why removing the child is an injustice, not merely why it is likely to be a bad policy.

Another strategy for blocking the BAP is to say that children only have a claim to a threshold of care, which would imply that Paul is not wronged by being cared for by Olivia even if Quinn would be an even better parent. Colin Macleod writes:

> This view [a child-centric understanding of parental rights] is often thought to be vulnerable to the objection that it implausibly authorizes assigning parental rights to the adults who are best able to promote the interests of specific children. This raises the ugly spectre, at least in principle, of redistributing children from adults who would be good parents to adults who would be better parents. However, I believe that the concern is misplaced ... The redistribution objection only arises in a troubling way if we assume that children have a claim to be raised in a way that *maximally* promotes their interests. (2015: 230)

However, while Macleod's suggestion that children only have a right to a threshold of care is plausible, he is wrong to think this suggestion blocks the BAP. This is because while children may only have a *right* to a threshold standard of care, they clearly have an *interest* in care which is better than this. By analogy, consider that in liberal societies people have a right to a lawyer to represent them in court. Presumably, we believe that people only have a right to a good enough lawyer, not to the best possible lawyer. However, suppose that Robert needs legal representation, that Steve is available and meets the threshold of adequacy, but that Tricia is also a possibility and is a truly fantastic lawyer. Also suppose Tricia is willing to represent Robert for no additional cost. It seems clear that, *ceteris paribus*, the state ought to assign Tricia rather than Steve because this better serves Robert's interests, even though Robert's rights would not have been violated if Steve were the only lawyer available. Similar considerations seem to suggest that children should be assigned to the person best placed to promote their interests even if their biological parents meet the adequacy standard of care to which children have a right.

Therefore, thinking through the BAP suggests that there must be some pre-existing moral connection between children and prospective parents, some reason why *the latter* are wronged by not becoming the parent. Taking the parents' interests into account is known as a dual-interest approach (Brighouse and Swift, 2014: 51). The task is uncovering which of Olivia's interests give her some claim to parent her child. Before outlining my own account of this connection, I consider three possibilities: genetics, relationships and conventions.

The genetic view

David Velleman argues that biological ties create shared characteristics and that these ground a special moral relationship between a procreator and their biological child. For Velleman, contact with biological relatives is important for children's identity formation (2005: 357–8). He argues that contact with biological kin acts as a kind of mirror through which children can learn about themselves. The biological connection also matters because it allows children to connect themselves to an ongoing story, providing meaning to their lives. For these reasons, he thinks that children's lives proceed much better when they are brought up by their biological parents and therefore children are wronged if they are denied a parental relationship with their biological creators. This position leads to a highly sceptical view of IVF treatment. He believes that 'What is most troubling about gamete donation is that it purposely severs a connection of the sort that normally informs a person's sense of identity, which is comprised of elements that must bear emotional meaning as only symbols and stories can' (Velleman, 2005: 362–3).

A demonstration of the intuitive force of the genetic view is the actions of (some) children created by artificial insemination. English paramedic Emma Cresswell went to court to change her birth certificate upon discovering that she was created by IVF, removing the name of the person she believed to be her biological father from the relevant section of the form and replacing it with 'unknown'. Cresswell is quoted as saying that she 'changed her name to reflect who she really was'.[1] Velleman's view seems well placed to make sense of cases like Cresswell's. Velleman's suggestion that people created by gamete donation lose access to a relationship which would provide meaning to their lives echoes Cresswell's statement that changing her birth certificate reflects who she 'really' is. The widespread resonance of the genetic view is also reflected in popular media and culture.[2]

Nevertheless, despite its widespread acceptance, the genetic account faces severe problems. First, it has counter-intuitive implications. It would appear to imply that people have duties not just to their offspring, but to anyone with similar genes. To illustrate, consider this case from Michael Austin. Suppose that Jeff has an identical twin, John, and that both men have a child. It appears, according to the genetic view, that each twin has an equal set of duties to each child, but this is intuitively incorrect. Instead we feel that each man has a greater responsibility for and connection with his own child rather than with his nephew or niece. But this greater connection cannot be explained by genetic similarity (Austin, 2007: 20).

The second problem is that there is reason to doubt the extent to which children's identity formation really does require interaction with genetic relatives. Far from supporting Velleman's view, Emma Cresswell's case is in fact seriously damaging to it because she didn't know she was created by IVF until the age of 26. By her own account, the thought that her social father might not be her biological father had never previously crossed her mind. But this situation would be extremely surprising if biology was as important as Velleman suggests; it ought to be easy to identify whether someone is your biological parent since the two of you will share so many qualities. Further, it appears that in situations where the biological connection is valued, children of IVF go to great lengths to find out more about their biological relatives, but in other situations and families this is not the case. Instead, 'adoptees who are brought up in families where biology is treated as one source, but not the only source for identity, are normally able to form healthy identities without contact with their biological relatives' (Haslanger, 2009: 16).

The final and most fundamental problem with Velleman's view is that it cannot explain why taking Paul away from Olivia would violate *her* rights. At most, it can show why Paul is left worse off because he has an interest in being cared for by his biological kin. While this would be an important conclusion, it cannot capture the sense that a deep wrong has been done *to* Olivia by taking Paul away. Therefore, whatever other merits of his theory it cannot answer the question posed by the BAP, which is why prospective parents would themselves be wronged if they lose access to the child. What is needed is an account of what Olivia has a claim to and why this is specifically a claim to parent Paul.

The relationship view

What I term 'the relationship view' has been most thoroughly developed by Brighouse and Swift, who believe the family is justified by the production of 'familial relationship goods'. This term refers to the benefits that people get from the family, like emotional support and shared identity, in which all children, and almost all adults, have a deep interest. They believe the protection of these goods justifies the practice of parenting as it currently exists:

> Even if a state successfully used orphanages to foster diversity and fulfil children's needs excellently, there would be a serious loss of value and flourishing. Many adults could not get access to the full package of these activities and relationship by becoming 'teachers' at the orphanages, because, in the role of teacher they could not enjoy the relevant kinds of intimacy with, or exercise the relevant kind of legitimate partiality with respect to, a small number of particular children. (Brighouse and Swift, 2009: 97)

However, while the relationship view identifies an important set of interests held by children and prospective parents, there are two problems with appealing to these interests as a way of justifying and assigning parental rights. These are that sometimes parents can have claims when there is no established relationship and that the relationship view struggles to assign a child to a carer at the moment of birth.

Parenting beyond relationships

The core of the first problem is that Brighouse and Swift's account privileges one aspect of what makes parenting important over other kinds of valuable parental activity and, as a result, their account misidentifies who properly counts as 'doing parenting' in the morally relevant sense. Consider the following case:

Long-distance parenting: Udita is a woman from India who moves to the UK because she cannot find work at home. She is legally permitted to bring her children with her, but she rightly believes they will face serious hardships if she does, including language barriers and potentially discriminatory treatment. She leaves her children in India and sends them a large proportion of her income. During this time her children are raised by a large group of Udita's friends and relatives and develop close relationships with these other adults. After ten years, Udita resumes direct care of her children, but for years struggles to develop a close and intimate relationship with them.

The relationship view rightly suggests Udita misses out on significant goods and we can reasonably imagine that she views her decision to leave as a significant cost or sacrifice. However, the conclusions of the relationship view are stronger than this. If relationships are what constitutes 'being a parent' then Udita is not really a parent at all, rather those people who have developed the relationship are the children's rightful parents. This implication seems deeply wrong; while Udita faces a regrettable choice, given the circumstances her choices seem to be an instance of parenting, not something that should mean she sacrifices her later claims to look after the children. Our intuitions about this case should be guided by the fact that her actions were done to benefit her children and that she may be right to think that they will be better off overall than they would have been had she stayed. This case focuses our attention on the fact that while flourishing relationships are highly important they do not exhaust the importance of parenting. We require an account of parental rights that can capture the notion of a 'good parent' (who keeps their rights) which is independent of the success of the intimate relationship.

A possible response from Brighouse and Swift is to suggest that I mischaracterized what counts as a 'relationship' in this case. Perhaps because Udita still loves her children she still has a parent–child relationship with them. However, Udita's relationship with the children lacks those features which Brighouse and Swift believes confer this value. She does not enjoy intimacy or spontaneity with the children, nor does she exert a deep influence over their developing characters. Indeed, we could alter the case so that the children do not even know Udita in any meaningful way because she had to leave them early in their lives. While one could define 'relationship' in such a capacious way that it captures even cases where the parties do not know each other, the example of long-distance parenting provides a powerful reason to accept that sometimes parenting can be done in ways which do not promote the kinds of relationship goods that Brighouse and Swift believe are what matters.

The right to start a relationship

The second problem with the relationship account is that it cannot provide an adequate link between prospective parents and specific children and therefore does not provide good reasons to reject the BAP. The problem is that even though procreators have interests in a future relationship with the child so do the other candidate parents. In my case, Olivia *and* Quinn both have an interest in parenting Paul because of the relationship goods that parenting confers. Thus, while the value of a relationship gives powerful reasons to think that existing families should be kept together, this value cannot explain why any particular person gets to start a parental relationship. What is needed to block the BAP is a reason to think that, at birth, some adults acquire the right to parent a specific child. This right would explain why other adults like Quinn would be acting wrongly if they tried to build a parental relationship with the child.

A novel and interesting solution to this problem is suggested by Gheaus (2012), who focuses on the moral importance of pregnancy and gestation. She believes that a morally significant relationship exists between the gestational mother and the foetus. Since children have an interest in continuing existing relationships, this implies that the gestational mother has a right to act as parent to the child. Gheaus argues that foetuses have a relevant relationship with their mother because they can recognize the voice of their gestational mother and that, on the mother's side, the process of pregnancy leads to a growing bond to the foetus (Gheaus, 2012: 449–450). An implication of the gestational account is that only mothers can hold primary rights of parenting. If the basis of parenthood is gestation, then only a person capable of gestating a foetus can be the primary recipient of parental rights. This denies an important principle, the parity principle, which holds that a child's parents have equal moral status. Kolers and Bayne outline the parity principle as follows, 'being a mother doesn't make a person more of a parent than being a father, or vice versa' (2001: 280).

While Gheaus' view is inventive, it must be rejected. The worry with her proposal is that she stretches what counts as the relevant 'relationship' between mother and foetus/infant. After all, the foetus is not even self-aware for much of pregnancy and never attains the sense of self that grounds relationships in the more usual sense. It is true, as Gheaus notes, that very young infants can recognize the voice of the mother and that this recognition changes behaviour, but these factors are not constitutive of a powerful relationship of the kind enjoyed by parents and older children. Thus, even if gestation does generate a relationship of the relevant kind, it is not true that this relationship's maintenance will have the same kind of moral importance that deeper and more mutual relationships do. In my case, if Paul was taken away from Olivia he might lose a proto-relationship that began in the womb, but he would likely soon form a similarly powerful relationship with Quinn. His interests in the relationship continuing thus seem much weaker than the interests of an older child in staying with their current parents.

A different argument Gheaus offers might resolve this worry. She also notes that gestation matters because of the burdens that pregnancy places on the mother. In virtue of these sacrifices, it would be unfair to deny gestational mothers the opportunity to parent the child that they have carried to term. I believe this is an important insight, but its relevance cannot be explained by the importance of the parent–child relationship. Rather, it is one way that parents act to protect their children and its relevance to assigning parental rights can be explained better by a different family of theories, drawing on the importance of the investments parents make in their children.

The investment theory

The investment theory was developed by Joseph Millum, who defines the investment principle as follows: 'the extent of an agent's stake in an entity is proportional to the amount of appropriate work he or she has put into that entity' (2018: 25). Millum situates this principle as part of a more general view about proper reward for the investments people make in an enterprise. As he says, 'it's my song if I wrote it, our bivouac if we built it, our amateur dramatic society if we founded it' (2018: 26). This suggests the central relevance of pregnancy is that it counts as *work* for the benefit of the child, not that it establishes a relationship between mother and child. A strength of this approach is that pregnancy would be morally significant even if the foetus was entirely unconscious and unaware of the benefits it was receiving from the mother.

The investment theory provides a good response to many of the difficult cases I have considered. It shows what goes wrong with the BAP, because a child's biological mother will have done a considerable amount of relevant work by the moment of birth. In my example this work gives Olivia parental rights over Paul that are not held by Quinn. It is these rights which are violated if the baby is transferred at birth. Millum's view also provides a plausible explanation for the example of long-distance parenting. While Udita did not enjoy a flourishing relationship with her children, she did put in considerable work to ensure their flourishing. Millum's view plausibly suggests this work secures her parental rights and that she would be wronged if after her return the other people raising the children denied her the opportunity to resume her direct parenting.

While I think Millum's view captures a good deal about what is significant in parenting, it has problems that mean it must be reconfigured. One worry is that he does not offer an account of who should have the opportunity to work for a child and thereby become their parent. Suppose that Quinn knows Paul exists and wants to become his parent. Knowing that her society follows the investment principle, she spends a great deal of time and effort making her home as well set up for Paul as it could be. This is clearly work that is intended to benefit Paul. Nevertheless, this work does not seem to give her any claim to become Paul's parent. When someone who is not already a child's parent does work to benefit the child, their work seems morally irrelevant. Millum argues that the reason is that work done to benefit people who already have parents does not count in the proper way, thus any work Quinn does will not count as investment because of Olivia's prior rights. However, this means that Millum's view will also imply that gestation is centrally important in establishing parental rights, indeed, it is the *only* factor that differentiates Olivia from Quinn. Just like Gheaus' view, this means that fathers only gain parental rights in virtue of any work they do to support the mother during pregnancy and after birth. While both Gheaus and Millum accept this implication of their view, I believe it is seriously counter-intuitive to suggest there is no such thing as a presumptive right to be a father. For instance, in cases of family separation it seems intuitively important to show why men have some rights of access or contact provided they are not guilty of wrongdoing or a risk to the child.

A larger problem is that investment cannot properly account for the *strength* of the presumptive right to parent. Suppose that we grant that Olivia has parental rights over Paul which she gained by virtue of her work in pregnancy and that Quinn has no such rights. These rights do explain how Olivia can be harmed by not being the parent, but on this account the magnitude of this harm is far too small. On the investment principle Olivia's moral stake in Paul is proportional to the work she has put in, so nine months of reasonably burdensome time. The harm to her is done by effectively stealing this time and labour. The harm done to Olivia by taking away Paul is thus seen as comparable to other cases where someone has expended months of time and lost the end product, perhaps building a motorbike or working an allotment. However, the harm done to people in cases like these is nothing like what we feel would happen to someone who had their children stolen from them. Any account of the morality of parenting must capture the intuitive sense not just that there is a presumptive right to parent, but that there is an incredibly strong right to do so. The amount of work it takes to create a baby is not enough to explain the enormous significance of the presumptive right due to which we feel that taking children away from biological parents and giving them to third parties is an immense wrong.

The project view

This discussion has shown why existing views fail to explain how a person can come to be connected to a child before their birth and why this connection is so important. I believe these problems can be resolved by what I term the 'project view' of parental rights. The project view rests on the general moral principle that we have a right to initiate projects using our own powers and abilities so long as these projects do not harm others, and that our ability to initiate and continue such projects is central to our flourishing. Returning to the view of well-being outlined earlier in the book, it is through purposeful projects that we realize the goods of agency and creativity. We have a special right to continue these projects once we have made choices and sacrifices explained by the existence of the project. This implies the existence of various rights which give people confidence to feel that if they decide to embark on a project they will have the ability to pursue it to fruition. In this instance, the claim is that the freedom to become a parent, if one chooses to do so, is extremely valuable for people generally and that securely having this freedom means that such people must have a presumptive right to the children they create unless they fail in some serious way.[3]

Like the relationship view, the project view builds on the fact that parenting is a highly important source of value to many people. I do though admit many other permissible reasons to want to become parents. Some people will just want to experience a nurturing relationship. But others might want to be integral to the process of creating a new life, perhaps one genetically similar to themselves. Yet others might care about their legacy. There are many morally permissible reasons to want to become parents and a person's interest in agency means the reasons why they choose to procreate are, at least in large part, up to them. People's lives go better when they have the secure right to parent – meaning they will be able to parent any child they create absent reasonably serious harm – and this widespread interest justifies a general right to parent.

A powerful advantage of the project view explains why prospective parents have rights over a *specific* child, rather than merely to look after any child. When one's projects involve the creation of some good or entity, then the control rights that go along with this project are to that entity, not to something equivalent or similar. If I paint a picture then I gain rights to *that* picture. By being its author I have rights of control over *this* book. In the case of procreation and parenting, this view gives a person rights to the very child that their plans and actions have created. Paul only exists because of actions taken by Olivia and Neil. Their right to embark on the project of parenting is the reason for his existence, especially if (as seems likely) they would not have procreated if they did not expect to parent the child. This consideration also explains why Paul should not be thought of as harmed by his upbringing, even if it was true that a better parent was available. If Olivia and Neil did not have the secure freedom to procreate then he would not exist all.[4] On the project view then, Olivia has a right not merely to parent *a* child, but to parent *the* child that her actions have created.

The project view should be preferred to the investment principle because it can explain the magnitude of the loss when people's presumptive rights are violated. While I have interests in deciding what to have for dinner, removing some options from me does not wrong me very much provided I have others available; the costs to my life and ability to make my own choices is low. In contrast, preventing a person from becoming a parent removes a huge source of potential value from their lives and is something for which there are no good substitutes. It thus withholds from them the ability to set their own aims and ambitions and then carry these aims through to fruition. The project view can therefore capture the huge loss to Olivia. She decided to become a parent and used her powers to pursue this aim. If the state takes away Paul it would effectively have taken away her ability to do one of the things that gave her life meaning in her own eyes. This large loss to her plans and sense of identity, much more than the effort she put in creating Paul, explains why we feel Olivia is greatly harmed by the child ending up with someone else.

Another advantage of my theory is that it can explain why men can come to have weighty presumptive rights to parent a child. Men, just like women, ought to have the moral option to become a parent and should be able to use their own powers to pursue this project if they so desire and so long as their project does not infringe on the rights of others. The facts of human reproduction mean that biological fathers will necessarily expend less effort and time creating a child than do biological mothers. For Gheaus and Millum, the strength of a person's claim to parent the child is directly proportional to the amount of effort they expend and therefore women will almost always have stronger claims. On my view, while the difference in expended labour is relevant, it is not the only thing that matters. Rather, it remains the case that the male had the freedom to decide to be a parent, chose to exercise that freedom and was a necessary component of the causal story that related to the child. While the asymmetry between the sexes might matter in many cases, it does not support the claim that only women can be presumptive parents. Rather, men have a basic claim to be a parent of the child unless there are good reasons to believe they would harm the child in some way. This right would justify some kind of access or shared custody as a matter of the father's interests (not just the child's potential interest in that relationship), though of course this interest could be outweighed by relevant interests of the child.

Finally, the project view also offers a satisfactory account of how we ought to think about the case of people, like Quinn, who wish to become parents but cannot for reasons such as infertility. Such people are disadvantaged in a very important respect and thus have a claim to state aid to give them the option of becoming parents. This could take the form of giving them the option to adopt, but would also include aid to help them conceive their own genetic child if they so desired, since perhaps their aims include biological reproduction or pregnancy. My view thus gives principled reasons to support state funding for IVF or other reproductive technology. However, while Quinn has claims to state aid, she does not have any claim to parent Paul since he is the result of a different project and comes into the world with a moral connection to Olivia.

Conclusion

In this chapter, I first explored the view that parental rights are justified only by the interests of the child. I concluded that this would lead to the redistribution of children to the best available parents. This repugnant conclusion can only be avoided if a moral link can be established between prospective parents and a specific child. I showed why accounts based on genetics, relationships or investment were unable to supply such a link. I then defended the project view, according to which parental rights exist to protect the freedom of those who wish to embark on the project of parenting.

Notes

[1] See http://www.dailymail.co.uk/news/article-2699045/Woman-conceived-donor-sperm-wins-six-year-battle-man-thought-father-removed-birth-certificate.html.

2 Velleman notes that those who dismiss the relevance of biology should find Darth Vader's revelation that he is Luke's father a puzzling dramatic moment, met with the remark 'so what?'

3 A version of what I term the project view is defended by Norvin Richards (2010: 27–50).

4 This reply raises various complications and might seem to imply that children are never harmed by actions that cause their creation. I think that there are cases of what is known as 'wrongful life' in which a child is, overall, left worse off by her or his creation; for a discussion see Shiffrin (1999). I will also suggest that parents have extensive obligations to children that go well beyond not harming them. The 'no harm' threshold is only used here to consider whether the project itself is permissible and why children are not wronged if they are not looked after by the best carer.

10

Distributing Parental Duties

This chapter considers how and why adults come to have special duties towards children. By special duties, I mean those that go beyond duties all adults have to all children, for example, not to harm them or to rescue them from danger when doing so is not overly costly. I defend the causal account of special duties, which holds that parents come to have obligations to their children by creating them in a needy and non-autonomous state. I first show why the causal view should be preferred to the other leading views of parental obligations which locate the source of duties in: (i) genetics; (ii) voluntary choices; or (iii) social conventions. I then consider the most significant objection to the causal account – the 'too many causers' problem. I suggest this objection can be met if the account is reformulated to track moral, rather than merely causal, responsibility for creation. I show that there are usually good reasons to think that a child's genetic parents are the prime causes of his or her existence and that they therefore have the most extensive duties to him or her. It nevertheless remains the case that other people in society have special duties to the child because of their role in his or her upbringing. In Chapter 12 I explore this idea in more depth and show why many adults beyond a child's parents can come to have special duties to him or her.

Genetics and duties

I have already rejected the genetic connection as a source of parental rights, but perhaps biology can provide a good explanation of parental duties. According to the genetic theory, the fact that two persons have similar genes because of shared ancestry gives these people special duties to one another. Current practice supports this suggestion, since many societies require absent *biological* fathers to pay support to the mother to defray some of the costs associated with raising the child. However, the

111

moral basis of the genetic account remains somewhat mysterious. To say that someone has similar genes is simply to say that they have similar codes in their cells, but this similarity does not seem like the kind of thing that would generate moral duties. What is needed is a reason why we should care about shared genes, especially when genetic similarity is present but moral responsibility for the child is not: for instance, the potential duties of a father whose sperm is stolen and used to create a child.

Some defenders of the genetic connection have relied on an explicit appeal to intuition. Jeff McMahan considers the case of a child conceived from donated sperm. The child will die unless it receives a bone marrow transplant and the donor is the only person known to have the right blood type. McMahan suggests that he has the strong intuition that the father's genetic connection does give the man a special reason to help, but freely admits he can give no explanation beyond this (2002: 375–376).

Like McMahan, many clearly have a sense that biology matters and that people should care about their genetic children for this reason alone. However, this widespread intuition is somewhat suspect since it can often be explained by evolutionary and cultural factors that must ultimately be rejected (Millum, 2018: 40). More pertinently, I will show that almost all of the cases in which it might seem that biology matters can be better explained by the causal view. The reason fathers should care for the children they create is not because they share similar genes, but because the child exists because of the father's actions.

The causal view

According to the causal view, people come to have duties to children because they create them, either as a considered plan or by taking actions that they knew might create a child. The standard justification for the causal view is that people have an obligation to meet needs that they create (Austin, 2007). If a person injures another such that they need treatment then they have a special duty to ensure that the injured party receives treatment. This view justifies placing parents under special duties because they create children in a needy state, requiring food, shelter, love and attention. If children do not receive these goods they will be harmed.

While compelling, this argument can only underpin a very minimal set of duties. The issue is that while parents do create children's needs, their actions also lead to all the goods in the child's life as well. It is thus doubtful, except in cases of abuse or neglect, that the child was harmed overall by their parents' actions. To illustrate, consider:

Moderate neglect: Victor and Wendy choose to have a child, Xavier. They are initially very keen on having children, but later lose interest and leave Xavier to fend for himself. Their house is well stocked with food so he can meet his nutritional needs. His contact with carers at nursery meets his emotional needs such that he does not grow up with any mental health problems. While Xavier is often very unhappy, he also enjoys many of the features of his life.

Intuitively, this example seems like a clear instance of parents failing in their duties. However, it is very difficult to say that Xavier has been *harmed* by his parents' actions overall, since he would not exist at all if they had chosen differently. While his life is bad it is worth living. Fortunately, the causal story can draw on other ways in which causing someone to exist might matter morally. Lindsey Porter argues that a different kind of special duties arise when a person makes a choice on behalf of another. She gives the example of a person meeting a friend at a restaurant; they are pushed for time and the friend is running late, so they have to order on the friend's behalf. Porter argues that when choosing for ourselves, we are permitted to make any choice we like, including ones which are suboptimal. However, when choosing for another person we are required to choose well. It would be permissible, if foolish, of me to order something too expensive or spicy for myself, but I cannot rightfully make these choices on behalf of someone else. Rather, I ought to choose what I think is the best thing *from their point of view*.

What this shows is when we choose for another person we have a special duty to justify our choices to them and therefore a person might act wrongly to another even if their actions do not harm them. In the trivial restaurant example, suppose that the chooser decides on a whim to ask for something she knows the other doesn't really like even though her favourite dish is on the menu. Overall the chooser's actions have not harmed the other, indeed perhaps they would not get dinner at all but for the chooser ordering. Nevertheless, the chooser has no good justification for choosing suboptimally and thus the other has a valid complaint.

Porter argues that creating a person can be understood as a relevant instance of choosing for them. She writes,

> Causing existence is an instance of (potentially morally permissible) choosing for. When I make it the case that someone comes into existence, I am choosing for them to exist. Because there is no opportunity for a non-existent person to make her own choice, we can assume that this choosing for is permissible only if I do my best to choose well. (Porter, 2014: 197)

While the restaurant example is a minor and one-off choice, in the case of creation the obligation to choose well has major and persistent implications. Porter argues that 'whether the choice was a good one or not depends on my ongoing actions' (2014: 197). Only if parents provide a good standard of care for the child while she or he remains vulnerable can they be said to have chosen well.

Porter's view is thus better able to explain our intuitions about the example of moderate neglect. By creating Xavier, his parents made a decision which primarily affected him and was thus one which is only justifiable to him. Their later neglect means that they did not choose well and therefore acted wrongly. Thus, unlike the genetic view, the causal view can explain the source of parental duties that meshes with our broader moral thinking. Parents come to have special obligations to children both because they potentially harm them and because they choose for them. To illustrate the strengths of the causal view I now consider two alternative theories of parental obligation which can both be understood as arising from perceived problems with the causal theory. I show how these potential problems can be met and why the alternatives each suffer from more severe problems of their own.

Voluntarism and absent fathers

Elizabeth Brake offers two objections to the causal theory: (i) that it creates an unjust inequality between men and women; and (ii) that it does not mesh with our usual treatment of risky but permissible activities. She believes these objections provide a rationale for accepting her alternative account, according to which parental duties depend upon a willing decision to accept them. Both of her objections arise through a discussion of absent fathers. Her central case is what she terms 'involuntary fathers', referring to men who have sex while using all reasonable precautions but still have children. According to the causal theory, these men do have special parental obligations. In contrast, Brake (2005) argues that involuntary fathers have not done anything to indicate they accept the obligations of parenthood and as such they have no special duties to the child.

Brake argues that applying the causal view is unfair to these involuntary fathers, in so far as they are made to pay child support because of their initial choice to have sex which results in procreation. Mothers are given the option of terminating a pregnancy and thereby avoiding duties to the child, but fathers have no way to avoid obligations. In principle there are two ways that the situation of the sexes might be equalized. One is to give the biological father an equal right to decide whether to abort the child. If abortion required the consent of both parties then both parties would face the risk of having extensive obligations to a child that they did not want.[1] However, this proposal undermines women's claims to self-ownership and would give the man extensive rights to control her body. Thus, Brake believes that the only morally permissible way to create equality is to allow men to leave without obligations to the child, at least in the early stages of pregnancy.

Brake presents her argument as an extension of J. J. Thomson's classic defence of abortion rights, which rests on an analogy between a woman considering an abortion and a woman who wakes up strapped to a stranger who needs her organs for nine months to survive. Thomson argues that while it might be morally good of the woman to stay hooked up to the stranger, she has no duty to do so. She believes that this analogy is relevantly like abortion because the foetus needs the woman's organs to survive and in both cases the woman is at liberty to prevent another person using her organs for survival. Crucially, when making her case Thomson argues that women who become pregnant have done nothing that implies they have special obligations to the child.[2] Thomson believes that later on parents do have special obligations to children. This explains that while women are permitted to let a foetus die they are not permitted to let their child starve to death. In these passages Thomson seemingly endorses a voluntarist account of parental duties, writing that

> we do not have any such 'special responsibility' for a person unless we have assumed it, explicitly or implicitly. If a set of parents do not try to prevent pregnancy, do not obtain an abortion, and then at the time of birth do not put it out for adoption, but rather take it home with them, then they have assumed responsibility for it. (1971: 65)

Brake's strategy is to endorse Thomson's view about these matters and then to argue that the same logic implies that fathers have no special responsibility to the child until they have accepted this responsibility. In so doing, Brake is showing that Thomson's argument relies on rejecting the causal view, since almost all mothers (except in cases of rape) will have taken actions that make them morally responsible for conception. If Brake is right about this then it might appear that endorsing the causal view would undermine women's reproductive liberties, because this implies women do have a special duty to the child and therefore abortion is impermissible. Brake believes that those who are convinced by Thomson's view must bite the bullet, embrace the voluntarist account of parental rights and therefore accept that fathers can avoid child support.

However, admitting that women often have special responsibility to their offspring need not imply that abortion is usually impermissible, because there are many good reasons to support abortion besides Thomson's view. One might argue that women's right to bodily autonomy outweighs their duties to the foetus, or that the interests of a foetus are less significant than those of older children because of the former's lack of cognitive development (e.g. see McMahan, 2002: 65–74). Thus, it is entirely consistent to think both that the causal theory is true and that abortion is a permissible action, and that therefore a commitment to reproductive liberty need not imply a rejection of the causal account. If anything, the fact that Thomson's view gives men permission to avoid supporting their child should be a reason to reject her theory, not to accept this conclusion.

The second problem Brake identifies is that the causal view does not mesh with our usual treatment of risky but permissible behaviours. Brake highlights the supposed problem with an analogy to the way societies deal with driving. She writes: 'we do not call a responsible driver a murderer when the statistically unlikely but always possible comes to pass … causal responsibility should not be confused with moral responsibility, nor moral responsibility with an obligation to bear all of the costs of one's actions' (2005: 59).

In reply, Porter quotes Nelson (another defender of the causal view), who discusses a similar case, writing 'A prudent driver who nevertheless hits a pedestrian bears special responsibility for doing what can be done to succor the accidental victim; saying "but I was extremely careful" may reduce or even eliminate the urge to blame the driver, but the responsibility to help out remains' (Nelson, 1991: 55). These quotations suggest that in one respect the two sets of theorists are discussing different issues. Brake's claim concerns moral critique and censure, whereas Nelson (and Porter) are interested in the distribution of *costs*. These two questions are linked but often come apart. We might think that a driver is entirely blameless (and certainly not a murderer) but that they do owe special duties to compensate the victim. These duties are justified because the person took a risk that actualized and people have duties to ensure they do no harm even when they are acting permissibly.

Therefore, Brake is wrong to think that analogous cases support her view that people engaging in permissible behaviour have no duties of compensation. Nevertheless, the driving case does not support the view in which involuntary fathers must have an obligation to bear all the costs of their actions. In the case of driving, society has created a series of institutions that socialize the costs. While laws differ significantly between countries, all have some ways of socializing health-care costs and of making drivers pay into an insurance scheme to cover costs they incur while driving (and note that these costs can fall onto the driver when they act negligently). In the case of the safe driver who hits someone, this radically limits their personal liabilities to the victim.

The socialization of risk benefits all drivers, since it is much better to pay a small fee to an insurance company compared with massive medical bills if one is unlucky. It also avoids the unfairness if some people faced ruinous costs for acting precisely the same as everyone else. These same considerations for the socialization of costs apply to procreation. Many people choose to engage in heterosexual sex and Brake and Porter both accept that the costs of abstinence are too high to expect people to refrain from sexual conduct. Under such conditions there are reasons of both prudence and fairness to socialize the costs of procreation between all adults. Therefore, while Brake is misguided in her approach to involuntary fathers, her discussion shows why the causal theory need not require fathers to bear excessively heavy costs. Rather, there are powerful reasons to create a society in which people are able to choose to have sex without worrying about excessive financial penalties, an argument I explore further in Chapter 14.

Social conventions

According to Millum, a person gains parental duties by performing a transformative act which is widely regarded as being an acceptance of parental duties. While Brake suggests that people only agree to duties via voluntarily or tacitly accepting them, for Millum it is sufficient that the agent should have known that their actions would generate the duty. In the case of absent fathers, Millum argues that there is a well-established convention that biological parents ought to care for their children. Men should know this convention exists and therefore, by having sex, they are consenting to these possible consequences. Millum's view differs from Brake's because it is irrelevant whether the man wants to become a parent, nor does Millum require an explicit contract between the mother and father about the future care of any child. In our social context, the act of having sex is sufficient to incur a special duty to any child created. He defends his view via an analogy with Norman Daniels' discussion of why doctors are under a special duty to help others, even at moderate risk to themselves. He suggests that this is part of what a person consents to when they agree to become a doctor. Daniels writes:

> It is not, after all, simply up to the individual entering a profession to tailor-make a contract that suits her wishes. The

shape of the professional obligations to which an individual consents is determined over time through negotiation with society … this complex structure of morally required and permissible professional behaviours is not up for renegotiation by each individual. On entering the profession, the individual adopts the whole package, which has the wisdom (and biases) of a tradition behind it. (1991: 43)

What makes this arrangement fair is that doctors have other possible careers and should have known that choosing the medical profession would bind them to help others even when they are not on duty. However, I do not think that Daniels' view is a good analogy to parenting. In the medical case there is explicit guidance (especially the Hippocratic oath) on how doctors are supposed to behave. In contrast, the social conventions to which Millum appeals are unclear and in flux. While many people do indeed believe that biology matters for parental duties, many others do not. Because of this, the guidance offered by Millum's view seems troublingly unclear. Imagine a man living in a city in the United States in which casual sex is relatively common and in which most women regularly use sexual protection and have abortions. Does this man's citizenship of the United States mean that he knows that he will have to act as the father, or does his residence in the libertine area mean that the relevant moral community does not link biology and parental duties? At the least, it is not obvious which conventions the man is a part of and therefore which he should be affected by.

More widely, by relying on whatever social conventions happen to be in place in any society, Millum's view lacks the resources to effectively critique those practices. One important value of moral philosophy is to provide principled guidance about what practices should be in place. Thus, a full theory must offer some justification as to *why* biological fathers, rather than someone else, should have a special obligation that goes beyond mere convention. Only then is a theory able to differentiate a just regime of child support from an unjust one. This is not to say that social conventions are irrelevant to the assignment of duties; conventions play a vital role in fixing the content of unclear obligations and can supplement an underlying account of the source of duties.

The 'too many causers' problem

Therefore, the causal story rests on a plausible understanding of how someone might come to have special duties, better explains the relevance of genetics to duties and has important advantages over both the social conventions and voluntarist views. However, despite these strengths many theorists reject the causal theory because of what I term the 'too many causers' problem.[3] In essence, the worry is that if parental duties go hand in hand with creating a child there will be an implausible proliferation of duties and too many people will count as 'parents' to a child. Consider this case:

Matchmakers: Zach and Yasmin are both single. Their mutual friend Amy decides that they would make a good couple. She invites them both to dinner to set them up, they do get together and eventually have a child, Briony.

According to common-sense morality, Zach and Yasmin are Briony's parents and have stringent duties towards her. The problem is that Amy seems just as much a cause of Briony's existence as they are. Had she not introduced Zach and Yasmin, we can assume they would have never met and thus never procreated. Despite this, it remains highly implausible to think that Amy has the same duties as Zach or Yasmin.

Recognizing that it is implausible to assign parental rights to matchmakers, defenders of the causal view have tried to show how their theory can avoid these kinds of implication. Porter has argued the view of what counts as causing someone to exist should be restricted. Her theory only counts those actions which are 'strictly necessary' to produce the child. Causal responsibility is properly attributed only to a minimal set of events, which includes all, but only all, the events that must be specified in order for the outcome to be implied by the entire set (Porter, 2012: 69).

While inventive, Porter's defence of the causal view is unpersuasive since it is unclear why the actions of Amy are not part of the minimal set. Her argument is that we only need to specify that the parents could have met 'somehow', but this ignores the fact that a person's identity requires their parents to conceive at a particular time so that the specific egg and sperm that made that person come together. The conditions needed for Briony to exist are very specific and therefore only Amy's intervention could cause Briony to come to be. After all, it was Amy's dinner and it was her invitations that led to Yasmin and Zach attending it. Even if they could have met in some other way that would have changed the time of their child's conception, meaning that a different child would have been born. Therefore, Briony's existence does indeed necessarily depend on Amy's actions.

More generally, in cases of assigning responsibility for a harm, what matters is merely whether a person was actually responsible for the outcome, not whether they were a necessary cause. Suppose an arsonist burns down a house, but also suppose that there were lots of other ways that the house might have caught fire that day. The arsonist's actions are not part of the minimal set of things needed to cause a fire since it might have happened absent their actions. But this does not matter – all we need to know in order to assign blame is that the arsonist did in fact start the fire that led to the damage. In a similar fashion, if it is right to think of causing a child as creating duties, then all that should matter is actual causation. Even if someone else could have acted so that Briony came to exist, Amy was in fact the cause of her parents meeting. Taken together, these arguments suggest that a metaphysical response will not be able to solve what is a moral problem. The issue is not whether Amy is a cause of Briony's existence, she most certainly is. Rather, the worry is that Amy's causal role does not seem as *morally* significant as Zach and Yasmin's.

Moral, not causal, responsibility

I therefore propose a modification of the causal view: a *responsibility view* of parental duties. This view takes account of the fact that a person's liability depends on much more than whether or not they played a part in the causation of the problem. Consider again the case of a man whose sperm is stolen and used to conceive a child. The man is definitely a necessary part of the causal chain that creates the child. Had he not existed there would be no sperm and therefore no child. Despite this fact there is widespread agreement that this man would have no special obligations to the child thereby conceived.[4] Existing discussions have failed to appreciate that there are many other factors which also limit the liability of people; in particular liability can be limited by: (i) the later actions of other agents; and (ii) knowledge of the likely effects of one's actions. Once these factors are properly accounted for the causal view does not have the counter-intuitive implications that initially seemed problematic. To illustrate, consider this case:

Criminal matchmaker: Amy knows that Zach and Yasmin both want to assault someone, she invites them both to dinner so that they meet, because she thinks it would be fun if they did it. They later do assault a child, Briony.

Two reactions to this example are relevant. First, Amy acts wrongly and she bears liability in virtue of her part in the event. Secondly, while she is strictly necessary for the act to occur, her action is not as significant a wrong as that of those who commit the assault. Liability is further lessened when a person is unaware of the possible effects of her actions. Consider further:

Inadvertent criminal matchmaker: Amy has a dinner and invites her friends Zach and Yasmin. She is the only person who knows both as they live in different cities. Entirely unbeknown to Amy, both Zach and Yasmin secretly want to commit a violent act. They meet at the party and decide to assault a child, Briony.

In this case, while Amy is just as *causally* responsible – her actions are still a necessary part of the explanation for the event – as Yasmin and Zach, her moral responsibility is much lower; plausibly she is not morally responsible for the act at all. Allowing liability to be limited permits the causal view to deal with cases that otherwise prove difficult. For instance, IVF doctors, like matchmakers, act in a way which is a necessary condition of the existence of the child. Porter concedes that they are part of the necessary set of events needed for conception and that therefore they have parental obligations to the child. Indeed, her view does not provide the resources to show why IVF doctors are not just as much the child's parents as are the child's biological parents. While Millum does not believe that IVF doctors are parents, this is just because current social conventions do not make this one of the actions that confer parental obligations. His theory cannot show why conventions that assigned equal duties to both doctors and to the biological parents would be deeply misguided.

In contrast, I believe that what matters is that an IVF doctor's liability for the child is lessened because they act only in virtue of the requests of another. In many other instances, this serves to limit liability. On my view, IVF doctors do have some special duties towards the future child that limit their appropriate actions. They have duties because of their causal role and must therefore ensure that whoever comes to have the child is capable of looking after it. It would be wrong of them to create a child without knowing it would be well cared for. On the other hand, their lesser responsibility shows why they are much less at fault than the child's biological parents if the child's life goes badly.

The case of IVF doctors is useful in showing why talking about 'parental' obligations is something of a mistake for the causal approach. The 'too many causers' problem seems troubling because it is so strange to call a matchmaker or an IVF doctor the 'parent' of the child. But these other people might still have special duties to the child for similar reasons, just to a lesser degree. The causal theory thus suggests that the sharp demarcation between a child's parents and non-parents is misguided. As I explore in Chapter 12, there are good reasons to think that while biological parents have most reason to care about the child, many people have some special reason to do so. Thus, the special duties that were thought to apply only to parents in fact apply to many others.

Conclusion

In this chapter I have shown that the causal theory of parental duties should be preferred to the genetic, voluntarist or conventionalist alternatives. The importance of this chapter in the ongoing argument will be to show why parents – and perhaps many others – have reasons to ensure that children's welfare is met. These reasons will reveal why the duty to promote children's well-being, as elucidated in Parts II and III, does not apply only to the state. In Chapter 11, I explore how perfectionism applies to parenting; in Chapter 12 I show how it applies to non-parents and other third parties.

Notes

[1] This possibility is explored by George Harris (1986).

[2] This explains why the woman is hooked up to a stranger, rather than imagining a case in which the woman was attached to someone she knows and to whom she is morally connected.

[3] This problem led Joseph Millum (2018: 43) to reject the causal theory. Bayne and Kolers (2003), though they do not reject the theory entirely, do consider it to be severely damaged by the 'too many causes' problem.

[4] Similarly, even those who press the responsibility objection to J. J. Thomson's view accept that women would have no obligations if the pregnancy were forced, for instance see Langer (1992).

11

Perfectionism and Parenting

In this chapter I consider what kinds of things parents are morally permitted to do and, in particular, I show why the perfectionist theory defended in Part III provides a plausible view of parental morality as well as the role of the state in upbringing. I do this by considering three possible views concerning the extent to which parents have a right to shape their child's values. While parents' ability to do this has been overstated, it is undeniable that parental actions have significant implications for their child's future personality, beliefs and values. For many parents, sharing values with the child is one aspect of what makes parenting a valuable project. However, liberal theorists have raised worries about parents using their power over children to shape their beliefs. The three views are:

1. **Liberal parenting**: Parents are permitted to engage in value shaping provided their children are autonomous by the time they reach adulthood. They may shape values according to any views of the good that do not lead the child to harm others.
2. **Neutral parenting**: Parents are not permitted to engage in value shaping or to make decisions that affect their child based on their own comprehensive beliefs.
3. **Perfectionist parenting**: Parents are permitted – and required – to engage in value shaping to promote their children's well-being. This includes, but is not limited to, a duty to raise children who are able to act autonomously.

I begin by revealing the problems with both liberal and neutral parenting and showing how perfectionist parenting resolves the problems with these perspectives. I then explore what perfectionism requires of parents and how it operates when understood as a moral guide to family life.

Liberal parenting

Liberal parenting is the dominant view in the contemporary philosophical literature. Joel Feinberg's 'The child's right to an open future' (2007) argues that while liberal rights cannot apply in the normal way to children, children have a right to have their future freedom protected. They thus have a moral right to the prerequisites of personal autonomy. This right operates against the state, giving children a right to an adequate education, and against parents, giving children a claim against value shaping that threatens their autonomy. This implies that parents ensure that their children have a series of skills that enables them to perform many different roles in society and are cognitively and emotionally able to make their own choices when they are an adult.

Despite some significant differences between them, liberal parenting is defended by Eamonn Callan (1997), David Archard (2003), Stephen Macedo (2009) and by Brighouse and Swift, who are worth quoting at length:

> If parents transmitted their values to their children by making them take value-determining pills, bypassing all capacity for autonomous judgement, that would be bad ... If they achieved that outcome by denying their children access to alternatives ..., or by taking advantage of their hugely privileged position with respect to the child's emotional needs ... that would be bad too. The autonomy proviso, to be discussed shortly, addresses such concerns. There might also be things that are bad about the segregation of a society into overly distinct, familially transmitted, cultures. A concern for civic integration may yield a reason to mitigate the intergenerational transmission of familial pluralism ... There are reasons to deny parents the freedom to raise their children in a family culture of thievery, or of corruption or manipulation of democratic political processes ... Such cases aside, it may be hard to see what is troubling about parents deliberately shaping their child's values. (Brighouse and Swift, 2014: 162–3)

Brighouse and Swift list many possible objections to value shaping, but all of them fall into two broad categories. Either value shaping is bad because it violates a child's autonomy or because it causes harm to third parties. Their analysis, like that of other proponents of liberal parenting, misses another set of potential problems that can result from value shaping: the harm that the values might have for the child. A person's comprehensive values shape his or her goals and structure his or her interactions with others. They are thus a core determinant of his or her well-being. Whether parents are shaping their child's values in ways that are positive thus seems a central aspect of the ethics of value shaping. The problem for liberal parenting is that value shaping can have pernicious consequences for a person even if they become autonomous, which means that even ensuring that children become autonomous is insufficient to ensure that their interests are protected.

The stability of value shaping

The first problem for liberal parenting is that value shaping (either intentionally or via background socialization) tends to have lifelong effects *even among people we should regard as autonomous*. Consider the following observations: Christianity is by far the most widespread religion in the United States. In the southern states most Christians are evangelical Protestants, in some parts of the north there are large pluralities of Catholics. The number of Muslims in the United Kingdom has risen sharply in recent decades. People's political beliefs are sharply correlated with those of their parents, even in cases where their economic circumstances have shifted (Achen and Bartels, 2016: 233). These mundane facts reveal a significant point, which is that despite children having liberal rights, experience of living a pluralistic society and having education up to the age of 16, it remains the case that relatively few people shift their ethical beliefs. The result is that much of the belief set held within any society is explained by childhood and the differences persist into adulthood.

Brighouse and Swift implicitly accept the persistent effects of value shaping, even on children who later achieve the requisite skills to count as autonomous by their standard. We can see this in the way that they prohibit parents passing on views that harm others as well as the autonomy proviso. The fact that they do think there are constraints on value shaping for other-regarding reasons show that they acknowledge the powerful effect that upbringing has. We should worry about parents encouraging thievery or racism because these are more likely to produce thieves or racist adults. The worry is that just as there are reasons to worry about the values children learn causing them to harm others, there are also reasons to worry about the persistent effects of value transmission on *children's own well-being*.

Non-belief components of well-being

The second problem for liberal parenting is that value shaping often affects more than just a person's belief set or his or her preferences, it also shapes the child's character, personality and skill set. These aspects of a person can be extremely significant for his or her current and future well-being, but they are not things which can easily be revised later. The problem for liberal parenting is that character shaping is both hugely important and often resistant to later autonomous revision. It is thus a way for parental influence to have detrimental implications for the child that cannot be negated by the autonomy proviso. Consider this example:

Language choice: Chen is born to Mandarin-speaking parents in an English-speaking community. His parents face a choice about the extent to which they want him to learn Mandarin as a first language. They might speak only Mandarin at home and ensure that Chen associates mainly with Mandarin speakers. Alternatively, his parents can ensure that Chen only learns English. Chen will have enough options to live an autonomous life no matter what his parents do but there are opportunities open to fluent English speakers and different but important values in associating with the Mandarin community.

The parents' choice here constitutes a paradigmatic kind of value shaping since it is intended to, and likely will, affect Chen's cultural commitments. Language is a useful example because people learn languages much more effectively as children. Choices made for a person during their childhood thus often have lifelong effects. While Chen will be free to associate with whomever he chooses, his ability to do so will be conditioned by his upbringing. He may never be able take on the speech patterns and confidence that comes with being a native speaker of mandarin and thus his ability to associate with some groups might be limited. Easy familiarity with certain cultural norms is also something that is difficult to just decide to adopt. For these reasons, Chen's upbringing will partially determine his later life even if he becomes autonomous and indeed even if he goes on to reject his parent's wishes about the sort of life he should lead.

There are many other routes by which upbringing can have such persistent effects. Some people struggle in some social settings and plausibly do so (in part) because of features of their upbringing. This effect could be intentional and again means that value shaping has persistent effects by operating on aptitudes or habitual behaviours rather than beliefs and desires. For this reason, liberal parenting wrongly discounts the potential harm upbringing can cause the child because it assumes that values learned during childhood can be revised later. However, people often cannot revise aspects of their character or skill set even if they wish to; therefore, a theory of justice should be open to the possibility that the values children learn can lead to bad outcomes for them.

Direct harms of value shaping

The final problem for liberal parenting is that the process of value shaping may itself harm the child *during* his or her childhood. Consider the following case raised by Brighouse and Swift. An Amish child is considering leaving her community, but the community makes it clear that leaving will doom her to eternal damnation in hell. Brighouse and Swift argue that the parent's decision to instil this belief in hell is wrong because it might compromise the child's autonomy, and that 'a religious upbringing in which one is psychologically abused with excessive fear of hell makes it extremely difficult for people to exit autonomously from a religious way of life' (2014: 172).

While I entirely concur that the children subject to this education have been wronged, understanding this harm mainly in terms of the effects on the child's prospective autonomy is a mistake. Teaching someone to believe, falsely, that if they act in a certain way they will suffer everlasting pain is a form of psychological abuse and is extremely bad for children, irrespective of whether it affects their future ability to make reasoned choices. Even if this child came to reject the religious views of their parents, and demonstrated full autonomy, there would still be a strong reason to object to the parents' actions. The child's upbringing has caused them immense emotional harm for years.

One might think that Brighouse and Swift could easily revise their view of value shaping to cover cases of abuse like this, so that 'psychological abuse' is added to the list of things that make value shaping wrong. The problem is that understanding why this case counts as wrongful depends upon making an assessment of the values that parents are trying to inculcate. Suppose that a child was considering using a dangerous drug like heroin. Her parents want to ensure that she is properly aware of the damage that the drugs can do to her body and, given that children (and adults) do not always deal well with statistics or dry data, try to make vivid the harms that drug use can cause by using pictures or video. These actions create an emotional response of fear in the child. But this fear would not properly be described as 'excessive'; rather it is one that creates an apt emotional response to the world as the child encounters it. If the child really would endure everlasting torment for making a few defined mistakes, then inculcating a terrible fear of these mistakes seems entirely justifiable. It is excessive precisely because this fear would be misguided in the case Brighouse and Swift describe, thus showing again the deep problems neutral moral principles give rise to when applied to the upbringing of children.[1]

Neutralist parenting

What I term 'neutral parenting' is articulated by Matthew Clayton. He applies the liberal principle of neutrality, as discussed in Part III, directly to the actions of parents. He argues that in order to protect the child's independence parents cannot intentionally shape their child's values according to any contested ethical theory. For instance, parents may not baptize their children or send them to a religious school (at least in order to make them more likely to accept this religious view). Beyond the religious case, parents may take no actions in order that their children come to hold any contested ethical view. Clayton's view avoids the problems of liberal parenting because on his account no value shaping is permissible and therefore there are no concerns with children's values being shaped in ways that are harmful to them. While I rejected the principle of neutrality as a constraint on state action, perhaps neutrality can offer a plausible account of parental ethics. The problem for neutralist parenting is that it wrongly privileges children's interest in independence ahead of their other important interests.

Clayton's account of what it would mean for a child to be independent draws from the Kantian theory of Arthur Ripstein, who writes: 'You are sovereign as against others not because you get to decide about the things that matter to you most, but because nobody else gets to tell you what purposes to pursue; you would be their subject if they did' (2009: 34). Clayton believes that a respect for children's independence implies that neither their parents nor the state may intentionally promote any contested ethical or theological values. Parents are required to raise children to be autonomous and to respect other people's rights but are not permitted to try and push their children towards any particular way of life. Nor are they permitted to refer to their own contested comprehensive beliefs when making decisions about their child. Following Ripstein, if parents make choices for the child then the child becomes their mere subject. In order to be properly sovereign and independent a child must make their own decisions, free from intentional influence.

However, Clayton wrongly proceeds from the fact that extreme value shaping undermines independence to the conclusion that *all* value shaping is a serious threat to the child. There are many mundane forms of value shaping that are entirely compatible with the child growing up to be fully autonomous and independent. For instance, some parents might wish to inculcate in their child a love of music, others sport and so on. While it is true that these parents are setting the ends of their child, it seems false to conclude these actions are a serious threat to the child's overall life. A person who likes cricket because their father took them to games hardly seems like the victim of indoctrination. The major elements of their life can be determined by their own choices, at least as far as is possible for anyone.

A more serious problem for neutral parenting is that it fails to protect children from being socialized into negative value sets. In objection to Clayton, Brighouse and Swift write that 'children's values are going to be shaped willy-nilly, by some complex set of agents with whom they interact, directly or indirectly (e.g. through the media). It's not as if the default is *no* shaping of children's values' (2014: 163). They are entirely correct about this, and the implication is that the choice facing parents is not whether to allow value shaping since such shaping is guaranteed. Rather, parents need to decide what values children will be socialized into endorsing. Implausibly, Clayton's view requires that parents make choices about children's environment without even considering the value of the ways of life that this environment will tend to promote. His view thus implies that it is morally wrong to make choices about where to raise a child *because* doing so benefits them by encouraging them to live well.

Finally, Clayton wrongfully suggests that parental value shaping is about pushing children towards a particular way of life. While some fit this model – perhaps raising a child in a particular religious faith – many parents only try and push their children away from things they consider empty or harmful. This kind of protective value shaping seems far less threatening to the child's independence than does pushing them towards one way of living. To illustrate these problems, consider the following scenario:

Parental choice: Two parents are deciding where to raise their child. While the parents will do all they can to raise critically aware and autonomous children, they know that the child is very likely to adopt one of the ways of life practised in the local community. One possible community practises four ways of life, A, B, C and D. The parents rightly believe all four ways of life are valuable and worth pursuing. The second community also practises A, B and C but also contains adherents of option E, which the parents rightly believe is empty and worthless.

Suppose that the parents decide to go with the first community because they believe it is better for their child. They do so because of judgement that option D is valuable, but that option E is not. For sake of argument I have suggested that this judgement is correct. Since they are acting on the basis of their ethical views, the parents' actions fail to meet Clayton's standard. Instead he requires that they make the judgement about where to live without considering the value of the ways of life available in each.

The fact that he requires parents to reason in this way opens his view up to the three issues I have outlined. First, it is unclear why the child should count as more independent if his or her parents did not make this judgement. In either case he or she would be socialized into one of four ways of living. Value shaping always takes place. Secondly, even if there were some reason to think he or she would be more independent, this gain for the child must be weighed against the possible risk of living in way of life E. Since living an empty or worthless life is extremely bad for the person, it seems unlikely that they are better off being slightly more independent but facing this risk. Finally, the case illustrates the distinction between value shaping towards one particular end goal versus protective shaping that merely pushes children away from bad outcomes. If the parents decided for their child that they had to live any one of the options this really would compromise their future autonomy. But all they do is push them away from an option and, as such, the child will still have lots of choice about how to live.

I believe the case of parental choice illustrates why neutralist parenting sets too many constraints on parents' behaviour. While parents have a duty to respect their child's future autonomy, they also have a duty to protect their children from living badly and this requires acting on the basis of their contested ethical beliefs. To link back to the discussion in Chapter 8, parents should be attentive to the risks of consumerist society or the homophobic beliefs of others. They should aim to raise their children in ways that prevent them coming to false ethical beliefs that compromise their future well-being. They should encourage their child to take up pursuits and relationships that will be a source of great value. This suggests that parents should act in a perfectionist fashion.

Perfectionist parenting and value shaping

Parental perfectionism is the view that parents have a weighty obligation to promote their child's well-being, including those elements of his or her well-being determined by his or her conception of the good. Parental perfectionism follows from the view of parental rights and duties developed in this part of the book. Parents have a weighty obligation to promote their children's well-being because of their causal role in their creation. Since a person's conception of the good is a determinant of their well-being, they thereby incur an obligation to ensure their children have a sound one. Parents' own interest in parenting is properly understood in terms of the success of their project. This should be understood largely, though not entirely, in terms of its *actual success*; that is, whether the children go on to live good lives. Following the arguments of Chapter 8, I believe that parents have a weighty but defeasible obligation to ensure that their children have a proper appreciation of nature, that they value their own and others' sexual choice and that they believe in profound scientific and historical truths. Parents should also aim to ensure that their children have a chance to develop their talents and powers of creativity. Actions that make children less likely to hold such beliefs and values or curtail their future opportunities to engage in valuable projects, are in one way wrongful.

Suggesting that parents should act in a perfectionist way is a revisionist idea to both family ethics and to the existing literature. Perfectionism is usually discussed in the context of what the state is required to do, whereas I argue that both the state and parents are each, for different reasons, obligated to try and enable children to live more flourishing lives. The same ideal of children's interests should, therefore, set the aims for both, though of course the kind of things that parents do is very different from what a state can provide. The idea is revisionist in family ethics since it more directly subjects parental choices to moral scrutiny than does liberal parenting. My account thus challenges the widely held belief that what goes on in someone's home is not a matter for others. Instead, perfectionism conceives of a child's home and other environments as important drivers of her or his current and later flourishing and thus a matter of public concern.

The implications of parental perfectionism: value pluralism

A serious concern with parental perfectionism is that it is overly restrictive and does not give parents any latitude about how to raise their children. This would be extremely problematic for my view, since I have defended the importance of parenting as a valuable option that adults might wish to pursue. Fortunately, while parental perfectionism does make moral demands on parenting it does not require all parents act in one 'correct' way with respect to their children. Perfectionism is compatible with a wide degree of parental freedom because of the existence of *value pluralism*. The theory of value pluralism that I referred to in Chapter 7 holds that there are many different valuable ways of living but that these values cannot be combined into one life. Each of the goods defined in Chapter 3 can be achieved in multiple ways and can sometimes compete with one another. Perfectionism is indifferent about which of the valuable paths a child takes so long as he or she ends up living one of the many possible kinds of flourishing lives. In addition, there are often powerful reasons from the perspective of the child to allow parents to influence which of these forms of flourishing the child goes on to enjoy. This is especially true when living one way of life allows for a better parent–child relationship.

To illustrate, suppose that a community supports only three different kinds of leisure activity: music, sports and art. Each of these pursuits enables different values and each can be an important component of a flourishing life. We might reasonably say that a life that doesn't contain any of these activities is impoverished in an important way. However, we should not think that a person's flourishing depends on engaging in a sustained way with *all* these activities. Rather, we think that a person's interest in leisure, and in developing their abilities, can be met by any one of these pursuits or by some combination of them. From this, it follows that perfectionism gives parents a moral duty to enable their children to access some of these goods, but the decision of which ones is entirely up to parents while the child is too young to decide for themselves. Moreover, parents are at liberty to encourage their children to take up an activity that they themselves enjoy *because* they want to share this activity. Parental perfectionism condones intentional value shaping so long as it preserves agency and other interests. Similar reasoning applies to many instances of cultural reproduction. Different cultural practices provide varying and often mutually exclusive paths to flourishing, and again the requirement is merely that the child live in one of the many ways that are compatible with achieving a good life. The perfectionist ethic has no objection to parents raising their child within a particular cultural form because of their own beliefs and because of their wish to share a life with the child, so long as this upbringing does not threaten his or her basic rights or undermine his or her well-being.

Similarly, one might worry that a perfectionist theory would require that all children be taught the truth about deeply controversial metaphysical questions, such that (for instance) there is no freedom for parents to differ on religious matters. However, this is quite mistaken. While children do have a powerful interest in knowledge, they also have a have a powerful interest in sharing a life with their parents that may include sharing a religious view (again so long as it does not undermine their interests). Children's interest in knowledge may well limit the freedom to pass on one's religious convictions, but the huge value many people gain from religious communities justifies a right for their continuation on a perfectionist approach.

The implication is that perfectionist parenting is much more hospitable to parental value shaping – even when this value shaping is in some sense suboptimal – than is Clayton's neutralist proposal. In many real-world cases my view allows precisely the same kinds of value shaping as does liberal parenting. Where perfectionism differs from liberal parenting is that it recognizes value shaping into an empty life is bad for the child even if it preserves his or her autonomy, and that this is therefore something that parents are under a moral duty not to do. Perfectionist parenting is thus mostly about avoiding serious harms to children rather than pushing them towards one 'best' way of living. Nevertheless, this remains an important theoretical difference because liberal parenting does not condemn parents for encouraging faulty values or beliefs except when such actions undermine a child's autonomy.

Conclusion

In this chapter, I have integrated the account of parental morality with the view of perfectionism outlined in Chapter 10. I have shown that it is not merely the state that has an obligation to promote well-being, but that parents directly have this duty. I have then shown how, despite the demanding nature of the view in some instances, parental perfectionism is compatible with a wide scope of freedom and delivers a demanding but not unreachable standard for assessing parental behaviour.

Note
1   Note the difference here between disagreement about world views and disagreements about values. Too often philosophical treatments of religious pluralism have treated society as divided on matters of value. While there clearly are relevant value disagreements, whether or not hell exists is not a value question. It is a question about the nature of the world, albeit one that depends upon issues of spirituality and faith in some respects.

12

Beyond Parents: Collective Duties to Children

In the final chapter of this part, I broaden the discussion beyond parents and argue that many other people in society have special duties towards children. The result is that while parents retain the principal role, the upbringing of children should be viewed less as an individual matter conducted discretely by parents and more as a shared enterprise among all members of society. A potential problem with much of the existing philosophical literature is that the field of family ethics is almost entirely dominated by discussions of parent–child relations. The result is that there is a large literature on the effects that parents have on children, and on the effects that the state might have (chiefly through its education policies), but a dearth on the effects that other actors might have. This is a serious lacuna in the discussion, since there is some powerful empirical evidence to suggest that the practices of children's neighbours and peer groups and the advertising they encounter are profound drivers of their later choices and therefore their flourishing (for evidence of the importance of advertising see Cook [2004]).

The empirical case against parental determinism

Parental determinism can be defined as the view that parents are the central determinants of a child's later personality and character (Furedi, 2002: 68). The implication is that had parents chosen differently, the child's life, indeed the person they become, would be entirely different. Countless books and magazines list hundreds of things that parents should do for their children, from 'baby superfoods' to the effects of Mozart on a baby's brain development. Philosophical discourse too sometimes seems to implicitly accept parental determinism. Lisa Cassidy writes that 'a child's life is utterly infused with his parent's parenting skills, both their aptitudes as well as their inadequacies. Being someone's parent is such an important endeavour that it is too important to do badly, or even just inadequately' (2006: 49). Both popular culture and philosophical discourse suggest a picture in which mundane actions by parents have huge and lifelong implications for their child.

However, in recent years behavioural psychologists and other social scientists have cast severe doubt on parental determinism. Using a variety of different methodologies, these researchers have tried to unpack the extent to which different factors impact upon a child's development. While the body of research is multifaceted and complex, reports on their findings suggest that in many instances parents matter a great deal less than the popular discourse might suggest. All the differences between the kinds of things that most reasonably well-off parents do do not seem to have much impact across a variety of metrics.

In its own terms, behaviour research aims to unpack the effects of three broad categories on children's outcomes. These are: (i) genetic effects; (ii) the effects of parents and home life, which are termed 'shared environment', because such are shared between all the children in any given home; and (iii) the so-called 'non-shared' or 'unique' environment, which includes any environmental factor not part of the shared environment. The aim of the research is to estimate the extent to which variation between children can be explained by each of these categories. For instance, if genetic differences explain most differences between children, then we should expect people with similar genes to tend to behave similarly in important ways, whereas if environmental factors are more significant then we should expect people who live in similar environments to show similarities.

In these terms, parental determinism can be understood as the thesis that the 'shared environment' explains a large proportion of variation between children, meaning that children raised by the same parents would grow up to be similar, whereas children raised by different families would grow up very differently. Suppose it were true that whether or not parents encouraged their children at school was the central driver of children's academic performance. This would entail that the vast majority of children raised by parents who encouraged them would do well and the vast majority of those who did poorly would not have experienced much, if any, encouragement.

The consensus of research is not at all favourable to the predictions of parental determinism. Instead, 'The effects of shared environment are small (less than 10 percent of the variance), often not statistically significant, often not replicated in other studies, and often a big fat zero

(Pinker, 2002: 379). Bryan Caplan summarizes the case against parental determinism as coming 'from disparate fields: medicine, psychology, economics, sociology and more. Despite their intellectual diversity and the ambition of their project, twin and adoption researchers have built an impressively consistent body of knowledge about the causes of family resemblance' (2011: 73). He believes that the consistent message is that there is 'barely a kernel' of truth in parental determinism. He surveys a range of outcomes that parents hope to influence, such as educational attainment or health, and finds that although parents have impacts while the child is young these effects tend to dissipate by the time the child is an adult. Again, I do not want to base any of my theory on the truth of these claims as they touch on expertise that is not my own. My point is merely that they are a stark claim about the nature of children's development and that if that claim was true it should have significant consequences for theorizing about justice for children. At the very least, the emphasis of the research should shift somewhat from thinking about the role of parents to thinking about what kind of social institutions and environments are most appropriate, or, perhaps one day, even considering justice in genetics (Fowler, 2015).

The point, of course, is not that parents do not matter for children's outcomes or that the questions of value shaping surveyed in Chapter 11 are irrelevant. Of course, there are myriad ways that parents must matter. The children of Christian parents are much more likely to become Christian than are the children of Muslim parents. When parents decide to move region or country, they radically affect the environment in which their children grow up. Finally, it seems almost tautological to say that parental actions matter for the health of the parent–child relationship, which is of intrinsic importance to the welfare of children while they are growing up and later in life. Rather, the point is that there is powerful evidence to suggest that within a relatively fixed context parents might not matter as much as we think.

In short then, the idea of parental determinism has come under serious scrutiny and combinations of genetic factors and children's socialization by peer groups and outsiders are now seen as increasingly important (see Harris, 2006). According to this view, parents' choices matter mainly in so far as they affect which peer groups a child will be part of, but, once an environment is established that includes other children, the decisions made by the child him or herself and by his or her similarly aged peers matter much more for later behaviours than do day-to-day decisions by parents.

To reiterate, this is not a book about psychology or sociology, and in general there are good reasons to want to avoid moral or political theories resting on contested empirical theories. However, in some cases appeal to empirical evidence is necessary since the normative debate already relies on, or presupposes, certain – potentially contested – empirical theories. By way of illustration, consider the ongoing debate about the permissibility of parents reading bedtime stories to their children. Adam Swift writes:

> Most evenings I read a bedtime story to my kids. I am showing a special, partial interest in my children. I know that reading to them gives them advantages that will help them in the future, advantages not enjoyed by less fortunate others. It is unfair that they don't get what mine do. The playing field is not level; our bedtime stories tilt it in their favour. (2003: 9)

This issue is also discussed by Mason (2011) and Segall (2013) among others. Each of these discussions seemingly takes for granted that things like reading bedtime stories matter a great deal, but this underlying assumption is precisely what is at issue in the research conducted by behavioural psychologists. The *New Scientist* quotes geneticists as saying that 'What confuses people is that there's a correlation between parenting and kid's outcomes. That's always assumed to be due to nurturing ... But parents reading a lot could reflect their own genetic propensity. When you do adoption studies, you find parental reading isn't causal.'[1]

My suggestion is merely that, given this school of thought, it is necessary to develop a position which is a bit less parent-centric. In the context of my theory, it would be problematic if I had convincingly shown why parents have strong duties to promote a sound conception of the good but failed to show why other actors had some reason to do the same. This would leave my view at the mercy of contested empirical issues, since if parents do not have the power to inculcate a conception of the good then no actor would be duty-bound to do so. As such, I aim here to show why similar, if weaker, moral reasons apply to non-parents.

Moral reasons for collective duties

I have argued that there is good reason to consider the morality of non-parents with respect to children, since there are good empirical reasons to think that the behaviours and choices of non-parents are often highly significant. It is worth restating the thought that empirical evidence of this kind cannot itself justify a duty to promote children's well-being. Whatever the facts about socialization or children's psychological development may be, they are morally inert and must be integrated into a moral theory to have salience. In this instance, we might think that non-parents have no special duties towards children because they did not do anything to create those children. Consequently, while non-parents must respect children's basic rights and not harm them, they would not have any further moral reason to change their behaviour in order to create a better environment. Within the larger theory, this would imply that while both parents and the state ought to be held accountable if children's welfare is lower than it might otherwise have been, justice for children does not make the same kind of demand on non-parents in their non-political actions. Against this suggestion I argue that all (or almost all) members of a society can be held somewhat responsible for children's existence, that influencing vulnerable actors incurs moral duties and that special duties to one child transfer to others.

Collective causation

In Chapter 10 I defended the causal theory of parental responsibility, which entails that people come to have special duties to children by creating them. There I raised the 'too many causers' problem, which alleges that the theory could count far too many people as parents because of their necessary role in the creation of children. I argued that the problem could be defused by showing that the causal theory should track moral responsibility and that (usually) a child's biological parents are considerably more responsible than anyone else for the child's existence. I conceded, however, that many individuals are just as necessary for that child to exist and that some of them may have duties towards the child on this basis. The fact that parents are most responsible grounds the common-sense view that a child's parents have powerful special duties to ensure the child's needs are met and should be held to account if something goes wrong. Here I explore the duties of third parties and suggest that many such people do have special duties when each of the following conditions apply: (i) they do in fact cause a child to exist; (ii) this causation is a predictable consequence of their actions; and (iii) people often do, and have reason to, welcome the creation of more children.

Establishing that many people are responsible for the creation of children is relatively straightforward. In Chapter 10 I considered cases like matchmakers or IVF doctors. These were useful illustrations of people not biologically related to the child but who are clearly necessary for his or her creation, but many other people fulfil this role. If we take seriously the thought that a particular child can only be conceived at a very specific time and place, then an almost infinite set of actions were necessary to make this child exist and thus any one of the people who committed these actions count as a cause. All members of society typically contribute to the existence of the economy and institutions like the health-care system that directly play a role in the creation of children.

Taken alone, the mere fact that many people cause children to exist does not seem very morally important, since what matters is moral responsibility. However, there are some grounds to treat people as somewhat morally responsible since the creation of children is a predictable – not an unknown – result of their actions. Introducing single people in their 20s and 30s is the kind of act that should be expected, not in any one case but across many, to lead to children. States that make various medical treatments available (most obviously infertility treatment, but any number of others) do so with the knowledge that these are likely to allow some people to procreate. More significantly, the cultural norms of any society play a central causal role in the creation of the children in that society. We can imagine a society that considered childrearing to be either morally wrong or a worthless enterprise and hypothesize that the rate of childrearing would be considerably lower than it is in contemporary societies where having a child is seen as one of the most significant causes of celebration. By engaging in a culture that celebrates procreation and parenthood people act collectively to make procreation much more likely in a way that is directly predictable.

Finally, many people *welcome* the creation of more children because of a child's intrinsic value and because of the effects on their own lives. As I will explore in Chapter 14, children sometimes provide public benefits because they will go on to become productive taxpayers who fund the pensions of people currently of working age. Quite what follows from this is a matter of some debate, but here it is enough to note that this often provides a reason for people to be glad when other people choose to have children. A second, more profound, reason to be glad about the creation of children is given by Samuel Scheffler. In his book *Death and the Afterlife*, Scheffler makes the case that our attitudes towards value are driven by the belief that the things we value will continue after our death. He makes this argument with a stark thought experiment and asks us to imagine a case where a person knows that a doomsday scenario will end all life on Earth days after their own natural death. He suggests that dwelling on this case suggests that while some projects will still have a purpose – those that give pleasure or comfort – in a broader sense life will lose meaning. If he is right about this then the meaning in our lives now depends upon the procreative activities of others.

In short, while it is possible to imagine someone who is very hostile to childrearing and procreation, for many people it will be true that they contribute to the creation of children via their direct action and by sustaining a culture that celebrates acts of procreation, and that they have reasons to want children to exist. The fact that an action which is causally important was foreseeable, and was welcomed, constitutes grounds to attribute *moral* rather than mere causal responsibility.

Socialization as 'choosing for'

The second reason why non-parents might have special duties to children is that by influencing a child's later character, third parties relevantly come to be 'causes' of his or her future self, that is, they are the reason he or she has the character and preference he or she does. Recall that the best understanding of the causal theory relied not just on creating someone in a needy state, but rather in *choosing for* another person. Creation counts as an instance of choosing for another person because the parents effectively decide that the baby should come into existence, but the process of socialization can also be understood as an instance of 'choosing for' in a way that would generate moral duties to the child as well. Consider the following case:

Suggestible: Ellen has a strange medical condition, such that she is temporarily in a non-rational state. In this state, she becomes extremely suggestible but only to the example set by her co-worker Fran. For the next year, Ellen is very likely to copy anything that she finds out Fran is doing. Ellen will later return to rationality but will find it hard to revise any of the beliefs or practices that she picked up from Fran. Fran did nothing to make Ellen especially vulnerable to her behaviour.

Imagining oneself in Fran's position would, I think, make most of us feel unlucky to suddenly have such a strong influence over another person, but, despite this, that we had an obligation not to pass on any negative practices.[2] The reason we would not want to have this kind of influence is that we are effectively making decisions for another person. In this case, Fran is *choosing for* Ellen, she is making choices that will affect Ellen's life rather than her own and this thereby incurs an obligation to choose well. Reasoning like this underlies the common belief that parents have a special responsibility to act as positive role models for their children. Consider a parent who lives an extremely unhealthy lifestyle. They drink too much, eat very poor food and never take exercise. Such parents are often criticized (frequently unfairly, given their possible options) not only for the effects of the lifestyle now but also because their actions make it more likely that the child will live a less healthy life in the future. Often this kind of reaction is restricted to parents, but passing judgements of this kind only with respect to parents implicitly assumes parental determinism is true. It would make sense as a moral practice only if children are greatly influenced by their parents but much less by others. If those who doubt parental determinism are right, and actually things like peer groups are the real driver of children's later decisions, as is the wider social environment of which they are a part, everyone who interacts with children stands in a relationship to them somewhat analogous to Fran's to Ellen.

The implication of this argument is that lifestyles which are entirely morally permissible for a person living alone might become morally wrong if that person is a parent or just in contact with children. The strength of this reason depends on the extent to which a person interacts with children, thus people who are known to be role models for children have a special obligation to act (at least publicly) in a way which is conducive to their welfare. Those whose lives keep them separate from children, and from those who influence children, may have no moral reason not to pursue lifestyles which are damaging to themselves (since they are under no duty to promote their own interests). However, those who are in contact with children must take steps to ensure actions that children will probably become aware of are likely to have positive impacts.

Intertwined lives

The final reason third parties come to have special duties to children is that children's lives are powerfully intertwined, meaning that the welfare of one child correlates strongly with the welfare of the other children with whom they interact. This is significant because it means that the special duties an adult has towards one child gives them added moral reasons to care about the welfare of others and the beliefs and values these others imbibe.

To explore intertwined lives, recall the suggestion that the central driver of children's socialization is their interaction with other children. The implication is that values and practices embraced by any one child are more likely to be embraced by others. Effects like this explain why there are social trends among children to buy certain products or listen to some types of music rather than others. If this suggestion is right, then in the language of political theory: (i) the content of children's conception of the good has a profound effect on their well-being; and (ii) this content is greatly influenced by the conception of the good held by other children. The implication is that rather than treat value shaping as a dyadic process in which parents attempt to influence the values of their children, we should instead think of it as occurring between groups of adults and groups of children. Various adults take actions, intentional or otherwise, which affect the values of some children and then those children's interactions with others transmit these values among a wider population.

To illustrate the importance of this change, consider the following case. Imagine there are three parents, each of whom is tasked to look after only one child. A looks after A★, B after B★ and C after C★. Suppose, first, that the welfare of each of A★, B★ and C★ is entirely independent of the others. Things which affect A★ will have no effect either way on the other children. Suppose that morally speaking, A's only responsibility is to promote A★ well-being. In this case, A should be entirely focused on the child in his care and should be indifferent to the fate of the other children. Each parent might rightfully think that the fate of the other children is appropriately the responsibility of their carers. With respect to value shaping, according to the argument of Chapter 11 A should try and shape A★'s values in ways that are conducive to their flourishing, but doesn't need to care (with respect to their role as parent) about the values of B★ and C★.

However, now suppose that the beliefs of B★ and C★ have as much or more impact on A★'s beliefs than do the direct actions of A. In this instance, A in *his role as parent* needs to care about the values and beliefs that these other children come to have. The potentially large importance of peer groups undermines the view that each parent's role is just to look after their own child and the lives of other children are morally none of their concern. The connections between children's lives means that to care about one child in society gives one reasons to care about the others.

A concern my argument here has is that it seems to imply that parents have a reason to remove their children from negative interactions with other children. Consider the following case:

Wall: A parent, Graham, has a child, Harriet, who is in constant interaction with another child, Ian. Ian has had a bad upbringing and has fallen into a way of life which is both bad for him and for the people around him. Graham has two choices: he can spend time and resources on improving Ian's care, which will improve his well-being and remove his negative influence on other children; alternatively, he can build a wall which will ensure that Harriet and Ian never interact.

It appears that Graham can meet his duties to Harriet either by helping Ian or by building the wall, but this seems like the wrong result. We ought to hope that Graham has reasons only to help Ian rather than to abandon him. In our world, many parents have taken many steps that have segregated the lives of (economically) better-off children from the worst off. For instance, richer parents have moved so that they are closer to schools which are perceived to be better, creating a division between schools attended by richer and poorer students. This separation is widely and rightly viewed as damaging to society as a whole.

However, this concern can be softened by taking a more nuanced view of Harriet's interests. As I argued in Chapter 3, people have a powerful interest in living in equal relationships with others. This interest is held by better-off citizens like Harriet as well as those who are worse off. Thomas Hurka eloquently captures this thought when he writes:

> Of course, each person's closest relations are confined to a few people, but he has thousands of less intimate contacts, and it is desirable if in all these contacts there can be some reciprocated sensitivity. If fruit vendors and bank tellers can deal attentively with him, he can deal attentively with them. Again, there is a point about overlapping groups. My closest friends will have other closest friends, who have other closest friends, and so on. For my relations with my partners to go best, those partners need interpersonal experience, which may require security and education for people I never know. (1993: 17)

In Chapter 3, I argued that an interest in social equality is particularly strong among those with whom one has close personal relationships. Deep differentials of power or status taint friendships and romantic relationships in a variety of ways, making one party subservient to another rather than relating to one another as equals, but as Hurka notes here there are similar – albeit much weaker – interests in our less important relationships having an egalitarian character. The implication is that it would not really help Harriet to wall her and a few select children off from others, who would then be abandoned to a low state of well-being. This kind of divided society might further her interest in more material resources, but, as I suggested in Chapter 6, our interest in material goods is not particularly weighty relative to our interest in relationships with other people. On a more holistic view of Harriet's interests, Graham's duties to her do indeed translate into a reason to care about the well-being of many children.

The importance of the entwining argument is to show why all (or almost all) members of a society have special duties to all of the children in that society. My first two arguments showed why many non-parents have special duties to some children. The causal process that led to that child's creation implicate many more people than just his or her biological parents, and those that come into contact with a child form part of his or her environment in a duty-generating way. These duties are then expanded by the intertwining argument. Whatever children a person has duties to will interact with many other children, so these interactions give the duty bearer a reason to care about the latter.

Conclusion to the parenting chapters

This concludes the part of the book that covers how people come to have rights and duties with respect to children. These chapters have played the following two roles in the ongoing argument. They: (i) secure the institution of parenting and delineate the scope of what parents may do; and (ii) show why parents, and other adults, have weighty duties to benefit children, including by changing their behaviour in order to increase the likelihood that children come to have a conception of the good that promotes their flourishing.

Parents have legitimate claims to look after children because it is important that people have the option to pursue the project of parenting, and because their actions are necessary to the existence of these children and were taken in order that they could act as parents. Since children will eventually benefit themselves from the option to become parents, all benefit from a regime in which all who are able to look after children to a requisite level have the moral permission to do so. I showed that parents have a duty to act in a perfectionist way towards their children, to promote good ways of living, but also argued that this duty was compatible with wide parental latitude. Value pluralism means that there are many different paths to living a flourishing life and, so long as children are on one of these paths, parents' actions are consistent with justice. In this way, the chapters have assuaged the concern that justice for children would 'crowd out' the legitimate claims of adults in raising children and in sharing their lives with them.

The second role of this part has been to move the argument from one merely about what justice requires towards showing the reasons that people desire to achieve justice. Parents come to have duties to children because of their central role in the child's creation, which counts as an instance of choosing for the child. This generates an obligation to choose well, which cashes out as an obligation to promote the child's well-being. Given the importance that a person's beliefs, values and character play in constituting his or her flourishing, parents' obligations to benefit a child translate into an obligation to be perfectionist parents. I then showed that the obligation to benefit children did not extend merely to parents and the state. Rather, other adults have several powerful reasons that require them to benefit children. The implication is that the principles developed earlier in the book apply directly to the personal conduct of all citizens.

Notes

1   See https://institutions.newscientist.com/article/mg24232310-800-the-parenting-myth-how-kids-are-raised-matters-less-than-you-think/.

2   Robert Goodin argues that vulnerability is itself a source of moral duty. In the case of childhood, he argues that the child's vulnerability to the parents is what grounds parental duties. Presumably if it were true that children are vulnerable to more adults this duty would widen in the way I suggest. See Goodin (1986: 70).

PART V

Distributive Implications

13

Children's Distributive Outcomes: Equality of Opportunity?

In this chapter I discuss equality of opportunity, specifically applied to the provision of schooling. The ideal of equalizing opportunity has immense importance in contemporary discourse and is embraced by figures across the political spectrum. In broad terms the principle requires that all children should have access to equally good schools and other educational opportunities and resources, and that laws and policies should aim to ensure that jobs and university places are not distributed preferentially to privileged social groups.

Recent research has shown that far from levelling the playing field, liberal societies are becoming more unequal in this respect. The current trend is a growing disparity between the economic outcomes of advantaged children relative to poorer ones. Thomas Piketty (2014: 22) finds that the proportion of wealth gained by inheritance has soared to a level not seen since the 1920s. Similarly, Robert Putman (2015: 190) shows that having wealthy parents is a better predictor of getting in to an elite college than doing well in early-year tests. However, despite seemingly widespread acceptance in public discourse, the theoretical literature has become increasingly critical of equalizing opportunity and has argued that it ought to be abandoned in favour of different (and weaker) distributive principles. In this chapter I show that these challenges must be rejected. I demonstrate that equality of opportunity matters because it promotes children's agency and relations of equality between children. In unequal societies, accidents of birth do far too much to determine a child's later life's course. While in Chapter 3 I rejected equality as the ultimate aim of distributive justice, in this chapter I argue that *economic* justice for children requires strongly egalitarian principles.

FEO and levelling down

The most theoretically developed conception of equality of opportunity is Rawls' 'Fair Equality of Opportunity' (FEO), which requires that 'those who are at the same level of talent and ability, and have the same willingness to use them, should have the same prospects of success regardless of their initial place in the social system, that is, irrespective of the income class into which they are born' (1999: 73). Society must neutralize, or powerfully mitigate, the effects of all social factors which influence a person's chances of getting a specific job. In the ideal case, whether a person has wealthy or poor parents should not affect their chances of getting any given job, nor should their race, gender or sexual preference. The only qualities that permissibly determine an individual's success are his or her natural talent and the amount of effort he or she puts in.

Taken literally, FEO is an incredibly radical principle. Applied to education policy, FEO requires that there are no meaningful differences in teaching quality across institutions. As I discuss at the end of the chapter, FEO has potentially even more drastic implications applied to children's lives out of school. There seems no sensible or permissible way to iron out all differences between children's upbringing and thus FEO can never be fully realized. Nevertheless, as I discussed in Chapter 1, sometimes principles of justice provide useful evaluations even when their requirements are unfeasible.

However, FEO has also been widely critiqued on substantive grounds, especially with regard to its vulnerability to the levelling-down objection. Deborah Satz writes:

> Suppose that some child's parents propose to devote additional resources to the development of their own child's talents. If the additional development of the child's talents enhances overall productivity, then this should, given appropriate social institutions, redound to everyone's absolute advantage. Suppose you and I are equal in underlying potentials, but your parents invest in special lessons and that leads your potentials to surpass mine. Although it may now be true that my relative position with respect to a given opportunity is worse, my absolute position may be better if your additional talent increases the size of the social surplus. It makes no sense to object to unequal talent development simply because one's own relative position is worsened. (2007: 632)

Anderson makes a similar argument. She believes that levelling down is a good reason to reject equality of opportunity and instead embrace the sufficiency approach. She requires that all children have a 'good enough' education but argues that there is no injustice with inequalities above this threshold. She writes: 'Parents who want to provide their children with more education than the minimal required to enable them to complete successfully a serious four-year college degree are free to do so ... The sufficientarian standard thus rejects "levelling down" educational opportunities to the lowest common denominator in the name of equality' (Anderson, 2007: 615).

Various implications follow from the proposals made by Satz and Anderson. For ease of analysis, I will focus most on whether, and when, there is any moral reason to restrict the ability of parents to spend money to improve their child's education. Most obviously we can consider the question of whether private schooling should be permissible. Both authors are explicit that their views permit parents to spend money on additional schooling to benefit their children. By contrast, private schools are a paradigmatic example of a type of institution that would be forbidden by FEO, since they are a way that a factor other than the child's own talent and effort comes to influence the distribution of advantages. For the sake of argument, I will assume that Satz is right that things like private schooling can boost the outcomes of some children without diminishing the outcomes of others.

Following this assumption, consider the following case:

Private schooling: Jim and Kate live in the same society. Kate has extremely wealthy parents whereas Jim's are poor. If private schools are permitted, Kate's parents will send her to a private school, giving her large advantages relative to Jim. The increase in her productivity resulting from the education she receives will mean that if the inequality is permitted Jim's likely income will increase.

Defenders of FEO, or similar principles, must show some reason to think that this scenario is unjust even though Jim gains in absolute terms. I first consider two leading arguments which purport to do this.

Unsuccessful defences of FEO

Positional goods

Brighouse and Swift argue that the levelling-down objection does not undermine FEO because educational goods are *positional* in character. A positional good is one whose value depends upon how this good is ranked relative to the others available. For instance, if only 1 per cent of the population have an undergraduate degree then this qualification will be extremely valuable, but if 50 per cent of the population have one its value is much less. To the extent that educational goods are positional, it follows that denying advantages to better-off children directly benefits the worst off. The two sets of children will later be in competition for scarce jobs and resources, and we are likely to expect the worst off to do better when rich parents are unable to pass on advantages, even when this has made no direct difference to the education the poor received. In the private schooling example, preventing Kate's wealthy parents from sending her to private school might boost the chances of poorer children like Jim winning a university place. Brighouse and Swift conclude that when it comes to education policy 'one does not have to be an egalitarian to have a reason to level down. Restricting inequality directly improves the position of the worst off' (2006: 475).

If Brighouse and Swift are right, then banning private schools will never be an instance of levelling down, since that means reducing the holdings of the advantaged *without* improving the lot of anyone. However, they are wrong to draw this conclusion. To see why, it is useful to add more detail to the possible scenarios and their effects on Jim and Kate. I provide some illustrative numbers to show how Jim can benefit from educational inequality even if the good is positional. For ease of analysis I have assumed that each person has at most four different opportunities and that the worth of each will be assessed by just two considerations. First is the overall value of the position to the person concerned, second is the chance of the person getting the job if they put a reasonable amount of effort into obtaining it. To say that Kate has opportunity A 100 (50 per cent) is to say that she has an opportunity worth 100 units which she has a 50 per cent chance of getting. The number 50 (80 per cent) refers to an opportunity that she rightly thinks is less valuable, but which she has a higher chance of getting. Here we can see the ways that permitting inequality might affect the opportunity sets of the two children.

Private schooling (specified) (S1): Jim and Kate live in a society which has instantiated FEO, so *private schooling is impermissible* and their opportunity set is identical. It is **A**, 60 (40 per cent) **B**, 50 (50 per cent) **C**, 40 (60 per cent).

(S2): *Private schooling is permissible.* Jim's opportunity set is now **A**, 80 (0 per cent), **B**, 60 (40 per cent), **C**, 50 (55 per cent), **D**, 45 (60 per cent). Kate's opportunity set is now **A**, 80 (40 per cent), **B**, 60 (60 per cent), **C**, 50 (70), **D**, 45 (80 per cent).

When we compare S2 to S1 we see that the overall value of the opportunities available to *both* parties increased. Kate has a much better chance at careers A and B, and these careers are of greater value. For Jim the shift is much less beneficial, since he loses any chance at getting option A, but nevertheless his option set in S2 seems better than it is in S1. The first-ranked realistic option is the same in both cases (which was A in S1 but B in S2), whereas the remaining two options are both better in one respect (either his chance of getting it or its value). By these numbers, moving from S2 to S1 *would* be an instance of levelling down. Brighouse and Swift's mistake is to focus on the competition for any one type of opportunity, rather than on a person's total opportunity set. While he loses out in individual competitions, overall Jim is not made worse off with respect to his income or the value of the opportunities available. Thus, revealing that educational goods are positional does not show that the levelling-down objection necessarily fails.

Self-realization

The self-realization argument for FEO is advanced by Rawls himself and later expanded by Robert Taylor (2004). Rawls writes:

> For it may be possible to improve everyone's situation by assigning certain groups powers and benefits to positions despite the fact that certain groups are excluded from them. Although access is restricted, perhaps these offices can still attract superior talent and encourage better performance. But the principle of open positions forbids this. It expresses the conviction that if some places were not open on a fair basis to all, those kept out would be right in feeling unjustly treated even though they benefited from the greater efforts of those who were allowed to hold them. They would be justified in their complaint not only because they were excluded from certain external regards such as wealth and privilege, but because they were debarred from experiencing the realization of self which comes from a skilful and devoted exercise of social duties. (1999: 73)

Rawls here explicitly allows for the possibility that inequality of access would encourage better economic performance. It is thus fair to read the self-realization argument as a proposed answer to the levelling-down worry. Unfortunately, while this argument does a good job of explaining why jobs and other opportunities matter in ways beyond the income they provide, it cannot defend FEO from the levelling-down challenge because it provides no reason at all to *equalize* opportunities. Consider the following variation on the private schooling case:

Unjust hiring: Jim and Kate are now 19 and candidates for the same position, which provides an excellent opportunity to develop various faculties and skills. Jim would be slightly better suited, but the committee eventually hire Kate because of connections she gained at private school. Jim lives off a generous basic income provided by his society.

Jim has been denied the ability to develop his faculties, and even though he has enough money to support his life from the basic income he might reasonably think he has lost out overall. Therefore, one might believe that the importance of self-realization to Jim is enough to show that the decision not to hire him was wrong. But this is not the case. If Jim got the job, then Kate would be the one to lose out on the ability to self-realize. The fact that Jim would miss out on an important good does not provide any reason why *he* should get the position rather than her.

In fact, far from providing a defence of FEO, if anything self-realization in fact provides a further reason to embrace the sufficiency alternative. Shields (2013) argues that the interest in self-realization is an interest that requires only that a person reach a threshold of resources. If he is right about this it follows that the state's interest should be in ensuring that all children have a good enough education to ensure they are able to meet this interest later in life, not that all have an equally good education. Matthew Clayton similarly argues that the self-realization argument, 'would seem to justify a distribution of educational resources that ensured that everyone had merely sufficient opportunity' (2001: 256). Therefore, neither the self-realization argument nor the positional goods argument provides a reason to value *equality* of opportunity.

Equality of opportunity and well-being

A better argument for restricting the ability of parents to pass on advantage is driven by thinking about the broader implications of inequality on children's interest. Inequalities of opportunity undermine important aspects of children's well-being, specifically in egalitarian relationships with others and in having the proper kind of agency. To illustrate why these interests comes into play, return to the unequal world described in the private schooling (specified) example.

Suppose that Kate ends up in whatever is denoted by opportunity A, whereas Jim ends up in whatever is denoted by opportunity D. The relevant question is *why* the children ended up in these social positions and the answer is to do with choices made by their parents and by the children's place in the social scheme. In contrast, in the society with FEO in place, the things that determine a child's later outcomes are his or her own abilities and choices. The difference for the children between those possibilities recalls a distinction I raised earlier, made by Rotter (1954), between a person having an internal rather than external 'locus of control'. Recall that an internal locus of control refers to the belief that you are in control of your own life and its course, whereas an external one refers to the belief that one's life is determined by the actions either of other people or by random chance. We can see in this example why, in comparison with someone like Kate, Jim could come to have a more external locus of control than he would in the world in which schooling were equalized. Research by Wijedasa (2017) suggests that disadvantaged children in current societies do indeed often think in this way. If social conventions determine that certain careers are fit for certain social classes, people justifiably have less sense that their own talents, personality and choices matter.

Another interest in play is the social relations between children. Suppose that Jim and Kate are fully aware of the options ahead of them and they entirely understand that the reason these options are different is because of their parents' social position. Critically, this means that children like Jim are taught to understand that there are some things they realistically should not aspire to do, or at least, when harbouring such aspirations, should know the odds of success are vanishingly unlikely. In this world, we should imagine teachers who work with poor children, making sure that the children do not follow certain role models – perhaps lawyers or doctors on TV – because, while those role models might look like them, their different social position means they are not appropriate people to emulate. This seems a paradigmatic instance of the kind of public inequality that would undermine people's ability to live as equals with one another (for instance, see Schemmel, 2011: 388). There would be a difference of *status* between the two children, reminiscent of that in the past between children of noble birth who should have one set of realistic expectations versus children of commoners.[1] A sustained acceptance of these variations in opportunity requires public acceptance that children from different social classes should have different aspirations and projects due to the status of their parents.

Alternatively, perhaps children like Jim are at least partially unaware of the extent of the inequality in their society. This kind of misunderstanding about one's options is common in current society. Gillian Evans quotes a report from a teacher from an inner-city primary school who said about her students: 'these kids don't know they're working class; they won't know until they leave school and realize that the dreams they've nurtured through school can't come true' (2006: vi). The problem is that these false beliefs directly threaten the agency of children like Jim.

Ben Colburn (2010) notes that part of what it means to have agency is to properly understand the options available and make choices given this context. Similarly, John Tomasi writes 'People are agents and their agency matters ... they have the capacity to *realistically* assess the options available to them, and in light of this assessment, to set standards for a life that each deems worth living' (2012: 40). The children Gillian Evans describes lack this capacity. They come to have unrealistic aspirations because they bought into the myth of equality of opportunity and were not properly cognizant of the impact their social position would have on which options were open to them.

Returning to the theory developed in Part II, people's interests in agency and social relations are often more significant than their interest in resources. Since benefits of this kind accruing to the worst-off count for more than those accruing to the advantaged, overall there is often a powerful reason to preserve equality. Thus, while inequality does bestow welfare gains on Kate there is still often a reason to restrict the ability of her parents to confer advantages on her because of the effects the inequalities have on Jim.

FEO and parenting

Thus far, I have only considered how FEO might apply to schooling. A potentially more difficult issue is how it applies to children's lives outside of school and to the conduct of their parents. There has been considerable debate concerning whether parents should be permitted to share activities with their children where such activities pass on economic advantage. For instance, many have discussed whether reading bedtime stories to children might enable them to do better at school (see Mason, 2011; Segall, 2013; Brighouse and Swift, 2014). FEO would seem to require not merely that children have similar schooling to one another, but also that they receive equal amounts of help from their parents. In Chapter 12 I surveyed evidence that suggests peer groups and other environmental factors matter a great deal for children's development, meaning FEO requires that children do not just have similar schooling and parenting but almost identical lives in every respect. This conclusion is obviously unfeasible, but, worse, is highly undesirable. Such a requirement would make becoming a parent overly onerous and would radically limit the diversity of lives that people could pursue in a just society.

In response, I will offer several reasons why FEO can be coherently applied to schooling without requiring implementation across all spheres of children's lives. One reason to believe that parents will usually almost always have a reason to read to their child or spend time with them at whatever cultural activities they wish, is that these kinds of decision probably do not make a huge difference to the child's later attainment. As I surveyed earlier, there are some who believe that the total impact on children's educational attainment of all the actions undertaken by parents is almost nothing. While I did not base my theory on this evidence, if these researchers are even partially correct we should conclude that the difference between spending time reading to children rather than, for instance, watching television is modest.

A deeper reason to think parents will be free to read to children is that my rationale for condemning inequalities of schooling does not necessarily imply that *any* inequalities caused by environmental factors are unjust. The core distributive principle remains the priority view, according to which gains to the worst-off matter most, but inequalities of well-being are not bad in themselves. Inequalities of opportunity are bad only when they cause disadvantaged children to be worse off than they otherwise would be. An advantage of this account is that it grounds the rationale for FEO directly in children's well-being and, as such, it can be weighed against the other contributors of the child's flourishing. I argued that FEO is good for children because it furthers their interests in agency and in equal relationships. These are powerful interests that will often trump an interest in more economic resources, as shown by the case of Kate and Jim. However, these are not children's only interests; some differences between children are required to allow them to have flourishing relationships with their parents while they are young and to have a secure right to parent as they grow up, as described in the project view developed in Chapter 9. The parent–child relationship is both a source of great value and much less likely to be a source of social division unless differences between parenting styles is caused by an inability of some parents to read with their children or spend quality time with them. As I explore in Chapter 14, I believe there are good reasons to ensure that all parents have public support to enable them to do these things and, in a more just world, allowing parents to raise their children in different ways does not seem to threaten children's sense of their own agency or their relations of social equality with one another.

Conclusion

This chapter consisted of a defence of FEO, in so far as I defended levelling down the opportunity set of the better off to achieve equality. I argued that the best justification for FEO is its connections to people's interest in living in a society without recognized social classes or hierarchies and in more accurately assessing the opportunities open to them. In short, the social context and relations between children provide good reasons to try and equalize the schooling children receive.

Note

1   It's worth noting that Anderson is herself as a relational egalitarian, thus my claim is that she does not fully appreciate the deep links between social status and opportunity when she defends institutions like private schooling.

14

Paying for Childcare

This chapter considers how far the costs of rearing children should be paid for by parents and how far the state should effectively subsidize parenting by paying for goods and services children need out of general taxation. This is a significant economic question because caring for children is extremely expensive. At a bare minimum they require food, schooling, health care and a dwelling for many years, and then there are the indirect costs of a parent's lost income, which are often even greater (Folbre, 2001: 34). The objection to subsidizing childrearing is that it is unfair to non-parents. I refute this objection by showing why an economic system that reduces the costs to parents is justifiable to all citizens because it makes a better option set from which to choose from when deciding how to live one's life.

The challenge: luck egalitarianism

According to luck egalitarians, a just society is one that mitigates the impact misfortune has on people's lives but not bad outcomes caused by their own choices. The theory requires compensation for bad *brute* luck (unchosen circumstances) but not bad *option* luck (disadvantages resulting from choice). Applied to parenting, luck egalitarianism seems to require that people who have children should internalize all the associated costs that occur because of the child's existence. Rakowski writes:

> Babies are not brought by storks whose whims are beyond our control. Specific individuals are responsible for their existence ... With what right can two people force all the rest, through deliberate behaviour rather than bad brute luck,

> to settle for less than their fair share after resources have been
> divided justly?' (1993: 153)

To illustrate the force of this thought, consider:

Different pursuits: Oprah and Peter want to have a child. They are
fully aware that this choice will require they make significant sacrifices
in terms of time and energy, but they believe these sacrifices are worth
making in exchange for the benefits of parenting. Quentin and Rachel
have an identical set of skills and careers but want to spend all their spare
money on travelling.

Luck egalitarians suggest the plans of both couples should be treated
alike in the sense that neither's project should be subsidized or penalized
by the state. Arguments in favour of sharing childcare costs across society
(pro-sharing arguments) aim to show why these plans are different, such
that justice requires subsidizing parents but not subsidizing travellers or
those with other hobbies or goals. I consider three existing arguments:
the 'public goods', 'kids pay' and 'socialized goods' arguments.

Pro-sharing arguments

Children as public goods

The most influential pro-sharing argument relies on the fact that
children are *public goods*, meaning their existence benefits everyone in
society. In order to have a secure pension, people like Quentin and
Rachel require a new generation of workers to pay into the collective
system. They thus require people like Oprah and Peter to have children
and to raise these children as productive workers. It seems reasonable
to think that everyone who benefits from children should contribute
towards their upbringing, since otherwise they free-ride off the activities
of parents. At base, this is an argument from fair play, which requires
people to pay into schemes of cooperation from which they benefit.
George (1987) argues that unless parenting is subsidized the activities
of parents will be exploited by non-parents. Folbre (2001: 50) also
believes non-parents have fair-play obligations to pay some of the costs
of parenting.

However, even though Quentin and Rachel do benefit in some ways
from others having children they do not necessarily incur a duty of fair
play to subsidize parents. On the most plausible accounts, the principle
of fair play requires that people pay into cooperative schemes they
benefit from if they *willingly* accept those benefits and understand that

contributions from recipients are necessary to keep the scheme going. To illustrate why receiving benefits does not always imply having duties to pay, Robert Nozick imagined a public entertainment system in which each member of a neighbourhood was assigned a day to plan and broadcast a programme. A crude rendering of principle of fair play appears to assign duties to a person who occasionally listens and enjoys these broadcasts. However, Nozick argues that this conclusion cannot be right as they never consented to join the scheme and they might rightly object that the benefits are not worth the costs (1974: 90–5). The people putting on the radio show are foisting costs on others, which they are not permitted to do even if they do confer some benefits.

Nozick's example might not be problematic for the public goods argument as applied to parents since children are necessary for the continuation of the state, which is a more formalized cooperative scheme than the one Nozick imagines. Further, following George Klosko, we should note that the benefits provided by children are much more fundamental than simple entertainment. The existence of children makes possible public pensions and health care, which protects people like Quentin and Rachel from an immiserated old age. Klosko argues that we can presume people would accept the benefits in question if these are of sufficient importance (1987, 2004).

However, while Klosko's argument is a plausible way of rescuing the theory of fair play in some cases, it does not work in the case of children. The problem is that people would choose to have children even *without* public subsidies. At the very least, it seems plausible that subsidies to parents could be considerably lower than they are now and there would still be enough children to maintain the needs of non-parents. This undermines the public goods argument in several ways. First, it seems plausible to believe people should only be required to pay into schemes when their payments are necessary to maintain the good in question. Secondly, it seems unclear that the activities of parents should be regarded as a *cost* for which they are due some compensation. After all, they chose to procreate, presumably in many cases because they believe it will make them better off overall, i.e. having higher wellbeing. Finally, the threat of overpopulation is often seen as worse than that of underpopulation, especially given the issue of climate change (Casal and Williams, 1995). Perhaps non-parents could be asked to contribute to the costs of raising children if there were an undersupply of children but, given that there is not, there is no public goods case for subsidy. Thus, while proponents of the public goods argument correctly note that parents benefit others via their activities, their mistake is thinking that this fact alone generates an obligation on others to contribute.

The 'kids pay' argument

According to the 'kids pay' view, Quentin and Rachel should have to pay some of the costs of parenting, not because of the benefits they *will* receive in the future but because of the benefits they *did* receive in the past when they themselves were children. They effectively owe society a debt for their own education and care and should discharge this debt when they earn money. The use of the debt is to create an ongoing fund to subsidize the activities of parents, and it is this use that ends up funding people like Oprah and Peter. At base, the kids pay view is also reliant on the theory of fair play, but this time it is the children who incur the obligations. As Tomlin argues, sometimes it is acceptable to foist costs on another, especially when: (i) the benefit being provided is necessary for them to have an acceptable life; (ii) the person is unable to consent to paying for the care; and (iii) it is unreasonable to wait until they are able to consent. All of these conditions apply to the aid provided to children by their parents and others, and thus it seems reasonable to foist these costs onto children.

A problem with the kids pay argument is that it seemingly enables wealthy families to 'opt out' of the costs of paying for things like pensions and health care. Suppose one set of wealthy parents fully internalized the costs of raising their children. They paid for all school and hospitals privately and did not take any benefits from the state to help their children. The parents also explicitly say to their children that they owe them nothing in return for this aid, which was provided freely as a gift. It should follow from Tomlin's argument that the children of these parents owe nothing to the rest of society to pay for pensions or other benefits. Thus, any subsidies paid to parents as a class should be paid by the children of poorer parents, not those of richer ones. This conclusion would be perverse, it would imply that children could grow up with significant unearned advantages and then pay less tax as they grew up as well *because* of having these advantages bestowed on them.

Tomlin (2013: 675) argues that his view can dodge these implications because he suggests that once a scheme of cost sharing is set up – in this case the scheme that shares the costs of raising children among those children as they age – it is appropriate to consider issues of fairness. He argues that for this reason parents who have children which are expensive to raise, because of their special needs, can rightly make a bigger claim on the parenting subsidies fund than can other parents. This is analogous to the way that some people have to make a bigger claim on society's funds for health or social care. However, Tomlin's response misses the issue caused by wealthy children. The worry is that rich parents don't want their children to be in the scheme at all. People become part of the scheme because they *accept* benefits provided by their parents, but if someone's parents choose to provide freely then we should not think of them as part of the scheme. Only if people are duty-bound to accept the benefits and pay into the scheme would his argument work.

Another set of problems for Tomlin is identified by Magnusson, who argues that parents are the reason that children exist and need to be cared for and that children are created because of the self-interest of parents. While it seems reasonable for a rescuer to make someone pay some of the costs of the rescue, this is not true when the rescuer is themselves the cause of the problem. In this case, parents cause children to exist and do so knowing they will come into the world in a needy state. Magnusson also shows that Tomlin's version of fair play is also undermined by the fact that, for most parents, the decision to create children is essentially self-interested and that it is unfair to make others pay for one's own self-interested acts (Magnusson, 2018).

Collective provision

Serena Olsaretti's view begins by noting that children are not, in fact, public goods in the technical sense of the word. Instead children are goods whose benefits have been *socialized*. In the economic literature, public goods have two defining features; they are: (i) non-excludable, meaning that it is impossible to stop third parties from collecting the benefits; and (ii) non-rival, meaning that one person benefiting from the good does not reduce the benefits to others. Clean air is non-rival because one person breathing clean air does not make the air less good for others, but many of the benefits of children described are not public in either sense.

Olsaretti (2013: 251) argues that children's future taxes are not public goods because society could decide to confer the economic benefits of children only on parents. She imagines a system under which all the tax revenues paid by younger people go into a special fund that only pays out to parents. Non-parents will have to rely on their own savings in order to fund their pensions or health care. While she does not think that such a system would necessarily be efficient, the mere possibility of something like this demonstrates why society should be thought of as *collectivizing* the benefits of children, intentionally conferring the benefits created by children onto non-parents. The taxes that children will later pay are an excludable benefit, it is a *political choice* who gets to benefit from these sources of revenue. Once children are seen as collectivized rather than public goods, it becomes more plausible to see why non-parents can be held as being under a moral duty to help pay some of the costs of childcare. Society has made a political choice to share the benefits of children and can justly require that those who benefit from this choice pay some back to support the parents who make it possible.

Unfortunately, there are several problems with Olsaretti's argument. First, it has some very counter-intuitive consequences. For instance, consider someone who is childless until the age of 50. It appears that this person would be ineligible for a portion of unemployment benefits or disability benefits until they had a child, but this seems unfair given that over the course of their lives they do just as much to help raise children as people who become parents at an earlier age. There is also some ambiguity about what it means to be a 'parent' in Olsaretti's view. Imagine someone who is childless but who does much to help her next-door neighbour raise a child. While they are not a parent in the legal sense, they have done much of the 'parenting' when this term is understood as labour expended to raise the level of human capital by looking after children. Since it is this activity which grounds the claim to pensions and future benefits it appears that many non-parents would have a claim to some of the benefits.

The larger problem underlying Olsaretti's argument is that it relies on the same kind of moral reasoning as Tomlin's. It sees people as being under a debt to pay back the benefits they got from their parents, and it is the payment of this debt which morally justifies the institutions of the welfare state. This way of conceptualizing intergenerational transfers is unsatisfactory. On her view, children pay into a cooperative scheme (the welfare state) but their payments into the scheme do not confer any benefits to them. Rather, people only get benefits from the scheme when they act as parents. This misconceives what the welfare state is about. Instead, we should see the welfare state as a scheme that allows each person to better distribute the resources available to them across their lifespan. They are able to lose resources during their productive life and have more resources available to them when they are either too young or too old to work (see Heath, 1997).

On this superior model children do not pay taxes to 'pay off' a debt to their parents, instead, they pay into a scheme today that will benefit them as they age, or if they become ill or unemployed. Under Olsaretti's proposals, non-parents could rightly think of the welfare state as something they need to escape or at least have reason to regret exists. From their perspective it becomes an institution they pay into but do not benefit from, rather than an institution that represents solidarity between all members of society. In sum, the core problem with both Tomlin's and Olsaretti's views is that it is not plausible or fair to see childhood subsidies as people paying off the costs of their own upbringing either individually or collectively through pensions. We need another way of thinking about distributive justice to show the moral rationale for sharing the costs of children between parents and non-parents.

Sharing costs for flourishing

In this chapter I have surveyed three leading arguments to justify the pro-sharing approach but showed how each failed. In their place, I will show how a justification for pro-sharing flows from the perfectionist theory developed earlier in the book. To best promote flourishing, society should create a basic set of institutions which ensure that people can become parents at only moderate costs to themselves, such that becoming a parent is a live and valuable option available to everyone. Making sure everyone has the option of parenting available to them furthers their interest in agency in two ways: (i) it gives people a distinctively different path to pursue if they so desire; and (ii) it better connects people's lives with their values.

Subsidizing parenting makes sense for these two reasons because parenting is the source of distinct kinds of goods which are not easily replaceable and it is extremely expensive when charged at a 'fair' market price. To see how expensive raising a child 'should' be at a fair market rate, note that Rakowski's argument does not only apply to things like nursery costs and child benefits. Rather, the ideal for the luck egalitarian is that *all* the additional costs to society caused by a new child are paid for by that child's parents. This means that parents would have to pay all the costs of schooling and health care their child incurs as they grow up. Becoming a parent is already very expensive and would be even more so if parents had to internalize all these other costs that are currently paid for by the state. While somewhat speculative, it seems reasonable to say this large price increase would mean having children would become unaffordable in the minds of many people.

The implication is that without some sharing of costs becoming a parent would not be a live option for many in society. Perhaps we might think this does not matter, because there are lots of other pursuits and goals open to people that are much cheaper, and indeed, in many cases, the loss of any one option does not matter very much. However, ensuring that people do have the option to become a parent does matter morally because parenting is the source of many distinctive values that cannot be effectively accessed in other ways. As I noted when I discussed the value of autonomy in Chapter 7, it is important that society provides not just a good number of possible ways of living but that these choices encompass a diversity of different values. The onus is thus not to provide ever more options, but to provide options which are distinctive from the others available and enable radically different ways of living and access to different goods. The ability to become a parent fits this criterion. It allows for challenges and experiences that are not available in other ways and connects with many established religious and secular views of the good. For these reasons, 'other intimate relationships have their own value, but they are not substitutes for a parenting relationship with a child' (Brighouse and Swift, 2014: 88).

To this, I add that being a parent allows access to special lifelong goods as discussed in Chapter 4, giving a relationship that persists across different life stages special importance through the change and development of character guided by both parties. While I concur with Brighouse and Swift about the distinctiveness of parenting, I do not argue that (most) adults are necessarily *better off* if they become parents. All I claim is that subsidizing parents gives people an option which is very unlike others they will be offered and which otherwise would be so expensive that it would crowd out many other important things in life.

Returning to the example of different pursuits, we can now see how these considerations show why the choice open to the couples with parental subsidies is more valuable than the one without them. In the world with no sharing of costs there would be modestly lower taxes. Both couples would therefore have higher income should they decide to go travelling, buy a better house and so on. But being a parent would be exorbitantly expensive and would either be entirely unaffordable or so expensive that a couple choosing to parent would have to make enormous sacrifices. The couples thus have access to lots of good non-parenting options, but the option of becoming a parent is not very attractive and may be unaffordable.

In the world where parenting is subsidized it is true that the couples would have a bit less to spend on other options. Taxes will have to be a bit higher, so there is less money to spend on their hobbies and projects. However, they can still enjoy many diverse lifestyles as a non-parent and these remain live and valuable options. The sharing of costs makes parenting considerably more attractive and means that becoming a parent need not mean sacrificing the pursuit of other aims and values, or living in immiserated conditions. In this world the people have a wider range of choices available to them. They gain one very distinctive and special option and still have a wide variety of other choices if they do not eventually choose to parent.

The second reason why subsidizing parenting promotes agency is that it makes an important choice turn more directly on one's values. The decision whether to create life, and in what family form, is a deeply personal one that will often reflect a person's deepest values and commitments. As such, it is one of the ways in which people become authors of their lives. They make choices that reflect and create the person they are. Valuable connections between a person and her choices can be blocked if the decision ends up being driven by things other than the values in question. For instance, consider other life-changing decisions like deciding to emigrate or to take up a different career. Suppose that a person decides to move to Spain because of their deep love of Spanish culture and cuisine and a settled desire to try and live in this way. This choice reflects and instantiates their values. Similarly, a person who had many options but chooses to become a firefighter or nurse because of their desire to help others acts on their ethical beliefs. Making such significant choices for oneself on the basis of one's own ethical commitments constitutes a particular kind of agency if driven by a love of a different country or vocation. However, this value is lost if the choice is driven by a lack of other options or by financial necessity.

In the world without parental subsidies, people would probably have to save money for many years, sacrificing other projects. Moreover, perhaps more people would have to take time off work to directly educate their children in the absence of free or heavily subsidized schooling. We can thus imagine many people who, while they would like to be parents and regard it as important, think that it is just not something they can do, given their financial circumstances. In contrast, in the world with significant subsidies, the decision to become a parent turns instead on whether one wants to have a child in one's life and the direct caring responsibilities this entails. In this way, the choice to become a parent in the world with subsidies makes the choice a better expression of people's values and ideals.

This kind of argument is much more justifiable to non-parents than are arguments which focus directly on how good it is to be a parent. People like Quentin and Rachel can rightly claim that they do not wish to be parents and that there are many other good things in life that are incompatible with having a baby. Nevertheless, it is true for them as well that their lives are better guided by their values when parenthood is an affordable option. In the world with subsidies, they had the live option to become parents but chose not to because of the importance of other things like travelling. The shape of their lives is thus directed by their commitment to these other things and thus they better realize the good of agency.

Thus far I have I suggested that there is a reason to subsidize options when: (i) doing so will raise the diversity of options open to everyone because otherwise certain valuable goods are blocked for financial reasons;

and (ii) the costs to the value of other options are relatively low (such that provision of the subsidies does not crowd out the possibility of a variety of valuable lives without taking the subsidy). Parenting is subsidized not because it is better than being a non-parent, but rather because it allows the realization of very different goods and giving everyone the option of becoming a parent means that a profoundly important decision is better connected with their values and ideals.

Parenting and work structures

In addition to direct subsidies for parents, like child support payments or free schooling, the structure of this argument can be applied to other ways in which society supports parenting. For instance, it shows why a just society must include laws that guarantee things like parenting leave or flexible working hours. The rationale for these laws is that they are supposed to ensure that becoming a parent can be combined with almost all careers and thus that a person does not have to give up their job or other projects in order to become a parent. In the existing literature, the usual reason offered for why such policies are justified is gender equality. In our gendered societies, in which women do most of the caring, a society in which becoming a parent was incompatible with working in many careers would effectively close off these careers to many women. The resulting gender imbalance would be bad for all women since it would perpetuate gender stereotypes about what kind of jobs women are able to do (see Gheaus and Robeyns, 2011). However, while this argument is persuasive, it has the odd connotation of meaning that the justification of parent-friendly working hours is *contingent* on the existence of injustice and thus not something that would be found in a just gender-blind society.

In contrast, I understand parental leave as part of the economic structure required to make parenting an attractive option. The costs to firms, and to other employees, of giving parents extra time off or flexible working is relatively modest and the result is that becoming a parent is compatible with taking on a much wider range of careers. The outcome then is that the option set available to all people across their lives is more valuable and that people's decision to become parents will be driven more directly by their feelings on raising children, rather than the decision not to be a parent being forced on anyone who wants to have a demanding career.

Conclusion

In this chapter I have demonstrated why justice requires subsidizing parents – and not just to the moral minimum. Rather, society should ensure that parenting is subsidized to the extent that parents have the ability to share projects with their children, and so parenting is compatible with a good range of career options. The reason for subsidies is not that children benefit others, though they do, but rather that distributive justice requires that everyone have a good option set available to them, including the option of being a parent, and that becoming a parent is not too costly to other aims or values.

Conclusion

The central arguments of this book have been that children are owed a good environment in which to grow up and that adults are owed the stable and supported right to care for children if they so desire. In Part I, I explored how to conceptualize children's justice and how to measure whether children's interests are being met by their society. I showed why children's interests cannot be understood in terms of holding a set of resources, even if resources are understood in a very broad sense. When the subject of justice is understood to be adults, then it makes sense that the role of principles of justice simply be giving each person their fair share. This was the perspective taken by the two most influential liberal thinkers of the last century, John Rawls and Ronald Dworkin. I suggested their approach cannot cope with the needs of children, since children might have a fair share of economic resources yet grow up socialized into beliefs, values and practices that are harmful to their current and future flourishing. A theory of justice must, therefore, take holistic account of the various ways in which upbringing might affect a person's life, thus looking at its effects on children's well-being. To meet this challenge, I offered an objective list account of children's well-being which suggested that this is principally driven by the quality of their relationships with others. This theoretical shift implies a reconceptualization of what justice is about. Instead of justice being understood primarily as economic fairness, it must be seen as fundamentally about creating a society with norms and practice which foster flourishing interpersonal relationships, with a particular concern for the least advantaged children whose interests must be given priority.

To meet this challenge in Part II, in Part III I considered what implications this shift of aims has for liberalism. I showed that the case of children provided a powerful reason to favour liberal perfectionism over theories of liberal neutrality. Perfectionism requires that the state promote well-being among citizens by making it more likely that they adopt a sound conception of the good. The attraction of this approach is that some of the most severe threats to children's flourishing come from the ethical beliefs of fellow citizens, especially the possibility that children themselves might come to adopt these faulty ethical beliefs. I discussed the damages of consumerism and gendered social norms as instances of ethical beliefs which do huge damage to the lives of vulnerable children. These are examples of ways of living that might profoundly constrain the kinds of lives lived by children who follow them because of the way they are raised. These examples were not meant to exhaust the implications of perfectionism. The point is to suggest a way of thinking about justice and children, namely that justice requires suppressing ethical beliefs because vulnerable children might adopt the views of those around them. The implication is that that many widespread beliefs and practices ought to be seen as at least somewhat unjust and that justice ought not be neutral on what a good life looks like.

In Part IV I discussed the implications of my theory for parents. I showed that the best account of parental rights is the project theory, which suggests that the reason people have the right to found a family is the value this option provides to their lives. Since on a perfectionist view the role of the state is to provide the conditions for flourishing, it is important to give people a secure right to parent, meaning that they would not lose their parental rights except under extreme circumstances. I then showed why the best available theory of parental duties is the causal view and that this implies parents have a stringent (though often non-enforceable) duty to promote their children's well-being, understood as promoting their ability to have flourishing interpersonal relationships now and later in life. The implication must be that parents are themselves under a duty to ensure that their child holds a sound conception of the good. I ended this part with a review of recent social scientific evidence that suggests the influence of parents on children is overstated and that peer groups and role models are central to the development of values and beliefs. I showed why this meant that all members of society had a moral duty to change their behaviour in instances when they were likely to influence children's lives. Taken together, these discussions challenge the dominant literature on children's justice in two ways. They highlight the excessive focus on parents at the expense of other actors and also show why existing views grant parents too much moral leeway to make decisions on behalf of their children. Children must not be viewed as merely parts of a 'family', but rather as separate and extremely vulnerable persons. Children are especially vulnerable to being socialized into ways of living which hold back their own potential.

In Part V, I explored the implication of my theory for two areas of distributive justice which are especially important for children: educational justice and parental subsidies. The central claim of my theory is that the aim of distributive justice must be to create an environment which is conducive to people living flourishing lives and that this aim is often not best pursued by sticking to seemingly fair market arrangements. In the case of education policy, I showed that permitting parents to pass on advantages to their children undermines poorer children's well-being and must be restricted. I then showed why generous support for parents makes a society an easier place in which to live a flourishing life. The result is to illustrate the moral rationale for a society, in comparison with contemporary Western societies, that is both much more egalitarian in its treatment of children and provides significantly more resources for parents.

To return to the questions with which I began the book, I have shown that children do not fit neatly into theories of justice developed for autonomous and independent adults. Because of our childhoods, all of us are profoundly dependent on others and intensely vulnerable to the ways that their actions influence our own lives. Seeing justice merely as the project of setting formal rules to govern the interaction of adults often sacrifices all but the most basic interests of children. Instead, we should see the just society as one in which people growing up within it tend to live good lives. The importance of this change is to collapse much of the distinction between ethics and politics – so fundamental to much of liberal theory – and instead to see politics as the development of laws, but also of cultural practices, that foster our ability to live well and to live well together.

Bibliography

Achen, Christopher and Bartels, Larry (2016) *Democracy for Realists: Why Elections Do Not Produce Responsive Government*, Woodstock, UK: Princeton University Press.

Ackerman, Bruce (1980) *Social Justice in the Liberal State*, New Haven, CT: Yale University Press.

Anderson, Elizabeth (2007) 'Fair opportunity in education: a democratic equality perspective', *Ethics*, 117: 595–622.

Anderson, Elizabeth (2010) *The Imperative of Integration*, Princeton, NJ: Princeton University Press.

Archard, David (2003) *Children, Family and the State*, Farnham: Ashgate.

Archard, David (2010a) *The Family: A Liberal Defence*, London: Palgrave Macmillan.

Archard, David (2010b) 'The obligations and responsibilities of parenthood', in David Archard and David Benatar (eds) *Procreation and Parenthood*, Oxford: Oxford University Press, pp 103–27.

Aries, Philippe (1962) *Centuries of Childhood: A Social History of Family Life*, New York: Jonathan Cape.

Arneson, Richard (1999) 'Against Rawlsian equality of opportunity', *Philosophical Studies*, 93(1): 77–112.

Arneson, Richard (2005) 'Distributive justice and basic capability equality: "good enough" is not good enough', in Alexander Kaufman (ed) *Capabilities Equality: Basic Issues and Problems*, London: Routledge, pp 17–44.

Arneson, Richard (2010) 'Two cheers for capabilities', in Harry Brighouse and Ingrid Robeyns (eds) *Measuring Justice: Primary Goods and Capabilities*, Cambridge: Cambridge University Press, pp 101–28.

Austin, Michael W. (2007) *Conceptions of Parenthood: Ethics and the Family*, Aldershot: Ashgate.

Aveline, David (2004) 'Parents of gay men and lesbians portray their lives', *Journal of Gay & Lesbian Issues in Education*, 2(2): 91–7.

Barry, Brian (1996) *Justice as Impartiality* (vol. 2), Oxford: Oxford University Press.

Basden, George T. (1966) *Among the Ibos of Nigeria: An Account of the Curious and Interesting Habits, Customs and Beliefs of a Little-Known African People by One Who Has for Many Years Lived Amongst Them on Close and Intimate Terms*, London: Cass. Abstract available at eHRAF World Cultures, http://ehrafworldcultures.yale.edu/document?id=ff26-006 (accessed 5 February 2015).

Bayne, Tim and Kolers, Avery (2001) '"Are you my mommy?" On the genetic basis of parenthood', *Journal of Applied Philosophy*, 18(3): 273–85.

Bayne, Tim and Kolers, Avery (2003) 'Towards a pluralist account of parenthood', *Bioethics*, 17(3): 221–42.

Begon, Jessica (2015) 'What are adaptive preferences? Exclusion and disability on the capabilities account', *Journal of Applied Philosophy*, 32(3): 241–57.

Berges, Sandrine (2007) 'Why the capability approach is justified', *Journal of Applied Philosophy*, 24(1): 16–25.

Brake, Elizabeth (2005) 'Fatherhood and child support: do men have a right to choose?' *Journal of Applied Philosophy*, 22(1): 55–73.

Brennan, Samantha (2014) 'The goods of childhood, children's rights and the role of parents as advocates and interpreters', in Françoise Baylis and Carolyn McLeod (eds) *Family-Making: Contemporary Ethical Challenges*, Oxford: Oxford University Press, pp 29–48.

Brennan, Samantha and Macleod, Colin M. (2017) 'Fundamentally incompetent: homophobia, religion, and the right to parent', in Jaime Ahlberg and Michael Chobli (eds) *Procreation, Parenthood and Educational Rights*, London: Routledge, pp 230–46.

Brighouse, Harry (2006) *On Education*, Abingdon: Routledge.

Brighouse, Harry and Swift, Adam (2006) 'Equality, priority and positional goods', *Ethics*, 116(3): 471–97.

Brighouse, Harry and Swift, Adam (2009) 'Legitimate parental partiality', *Philosophy and Public Affairs*, 37(1): 43–80.

Brighouse, Harry and Swift, Adam (2014) *Family Values: The Ethics of Parent–Child Relationships*, Princeton, NJ: Princeton University Press.

Burtt, Shelly (2003) 'Comprehensive educations and liberal understandings of autonomy', in Walter Feinberg and Kevin McDonough (eds) *Citizenship Education in Liberal-Democratic Societies: Teaching for Cosmopolitan Values and Collective Identities*, Oxford: Oxford University Press, pp 179–207.

Callan, Eamonn (1997) *Creating Citizens: Political Education and Liberal Democracy*, Oxford: Oxford University Press.

Callan, Eamonn (1999) 'A note on patriotism and utopianism: A response to Schrag', *Studies in Philosophy and Education*, 18(3): 197–201.

Campbell, Steven (2015) 'When the shape of a life matters', *Ethical Theory and Moral Practice*, 18(3): 565–75.

Caplan, Bryan (2011) *Selfish Reasons to Have More Kids: Why Being a Great Parent is Less Work and More Fun than You Think*, New York: Basic Books.

Casal, Paula (2007) 'Why sufficiency is not enough', *Ethics*, 117(2): 296–326.

Casal, Paula and Williams, Andrew (1995) 'Rights, equality and procreation', *Analysis and Kritik*, 17: 93–116.

Cassidy, Lisa (2006) 'That many of us should not parent', *Hypatia*, 21(4): 40–57.

Chambers, Clare (2007) *Sex, Culture, and Justice: The Limits of Choice*, University Park: Pennsylvania State University Press.

Chan, Joseph (2000) 'Legitimacy, unanimity, and perfectionism', *Philosophy and Public Affairs*, 29: 5–42.

Christiano, Thomas (1996) *The Rule of the Many*, Boulder, CO: Westview Press.

Christman, John (2009) *The Politics of Persons: Individual Autonomy and Socio-Historical Selves*, Cambridge: Cambridge University Press.

Clark, Sam (2018) 'Narrative, self-realisation, and the shape of a life', *Ethical Theory and Moral Practice*, 21(2): 371–85.

Clayton, Matthew (2001) 'Rawls and natural aristocracy', *Croatian Journal of Philosophy*, 1: 239–59.

Clayton, Matthew (2006) *Justice and Legitimacy in Upbringing*, Oxford: Oxford University Press.

Clayton, Matthew (2012) 'Debate: the case against the comprehensive enrolment of children', *Journal of Political Philosophy*, 20: 353–64.

Cohen, Gerald A. (1989) 'On the currency of egalitarian justice', *Ethics*, 99(4): 906–44.

Cohen, Gerald A. (2003) 'Facts and principles', *Philosophy and Public Affairs*, 31(3): 211–45.

Cohen, Gerald A. (2009) *Why Not Socialism?* Princeton, NJ: Princeton University Press.

Colburn, Ben (2010) *Autonomy and Liberalism*, Abingdon: Routledge.

Cook, Dan T. (2004) *The Commodification of Childhood: The Children's Clothing Industry and the Rise of the Child Consumer*, London: Duke University Press.

Cripps, Elizabeth (2017a) 'Do parents have a special duty to mitigate climate change?' *Politics, Philosophy and Economics*, 16(3): 308–25.

Cripps, Elizabeth (2017b) 'Justice, integrity and moral community: do parents owe it to their children to bring them up as good global climate citizens?' *Proceedings of the Aristotelian Society*, 117(1): 41–59.

Daniels, Norman (1991) 'Duty to treat or right to refuse', *Hastings Centre Report*, 21(2): 36–46.

Deaton, Angus (2008) 'Income, health, and well-being around the world: evidence from the Gallup World Poll', *Journal of Economic Perspectives*, 22(2): 53–72.

De Wijze, Stephen (2000) 'The family and political justice: the case for political liberalisms', *Journal of Ethics*, 4: 257–81.

Dorsey, Dale (2015) 'The significance of a life's shape', *Ethics*, 125(2): 303–30.

Dworkin, Ronald (1981a) 'What is equality? Part 1: equality of welfare', *Philosophy and Public Affairs*, 10(3): 185–246.

Dworkin, Ronald (1981b) 'What is equality? Part 2: equality of resources', *Philosophy and Public Affairs*, 10(4): 283–345.

Dworkin, Ronald (1990) 'Foundations of liberal equality', in Grethc B. Peterson (ed.), *The Tanner Lecture on Human Values*, vol. 11, pp 1–119.

Dworkin, Ronald (2000) *Sovereign Virtue: The Theory and Practice of Equality*, Cambridge, MA: Harvard University Press.

Dworkin, Ronald (2013) *Justice for Hedgehogs*, Boston, MA: Harvard University Press.

Easterlin, Richard (1974) 'Does economic growth improve the human lot? Some empirical evidence', in Paul David and Melvin Reder (eds) *Nations and Households in Economic Growth*, New York: Academic Press, pp 90–124.

Easterlin, Richard (2003) 'Explaining happiness', *Proceedings of the National Academy of Sciences*, 100(19): 1176–83.

Edlund, Jonas and Oun, Ida (2016) 'Who should work and who should care? Attitudes towards the desirable division of labour between mothers and fathers in five European countries', *Acta Sociologica*, 59(2): 151–69.

Elster, Jon (1983) *Sour Grapes: Studies in the Subversion of Rationality*, Cambridge: Cambridge University Press.

Evans, Gillian (2006) *Educational Failure and Working-Class White Children in Britain*, Basingstoke: Palgrave Macmillan.

Farrelly, Colin (2007) 'Justice in ideal theory: a refutation', *Political Studies*, 55: 844–64.

Feinberg, Joel (2007) 'The child's right to an open future', in Randall Curren (ed) *Philosophy of Education: An Anthology*, Oxford: Blackwell, pp 112–23.

Field, Frank (2010) *The Foundation Years: Preventing Poor Children becoming Poor Adults*, London: Cabinet Office.

Fishkin, Joseph (2014) *Bottlenecks: A New Theory of Equality of Opportunity*, Oxford: Oxford University Press.

Folbre, Nancy (2001) *The Invisible Heart: Economics and Family Values*, New York: New Press.

Forrest, Barbara (2011) 'The non-epistemology of intelligent design: its implications for public policy', *Synthese*, 178(2): 331–79.

Fowler, Tim (2011) 'The limits of civic education: the divergent implications of political and comprehensive liberalism', *Theory and Research in Education*, 9(1): 87–100.

Fowler, Tim (2014) 'The status of child citizens', *Politics, Philosophy and Economics*, 13(1): 93–113.

Fowler, Tim (2015) 'In defence of state directed enhancement', *Journal of Applied Philosophy*, 32(1): 67–81.

Frankfurt, Harry (1987) 'Equality as a moral ideal', *Ethics*, 125(4): 21–43.

Friedman, Marilyn (2002) *Autonomy, Gender, Politics*, New York: Oxford University Press.

Furedi, Frank (2002) *Paranoid Parenting: Why Ignoring the Experts May Be Best for Your Child*, Chicago: Chicago Review Press.

Gale, Catharine R., Batty, G. David and Deary, Ian J. (2008) 'Locus of control at age 10 years and health outcomes and behaviours at age 30 years: the 1970 British Cohort Study', *Psychosomatic Medicine*, 70(4): 397–403.

Gardner, Peter (1984) 'Another look at controversial issues and the curriculum', *Journal of Curriculum Studies*, 16(4): 379–85.

Gaus, Gerald (2003) 'Liberal neutrality: a compelling and radical principle', in Steven Walls and George Klosko (eds) *Perfectionism and Neutrality*, Oxford: Rowman & Littlefield, pp 137–67.

Gaus, Gerald (2016) *The Order of Public Reason: A Theory of Morality and Freedom in a Diverse and Bounded World*, Cambridge: Cambridge University Press.

George, Rolf (1987) 'Who should bear the costs of children?' *Public Affairs Quarterly*, 1: 1–42.

Gheaus, Anca (2012) 'The right to parent one's biological baby', *Journal of Political Philosophy*, 20(4): 432–55.

Gheaus, Anca (2013) 'The feasibility constraint on the concept of justice', *Philosophical Quarterly*, 53(252): 445–64.

Gheaus, Anca (2015) 'Unfinished adults and defective children: on the nature and value of childhood', *Journal of Ethics and Social Philosophy*, 9(1): 1–21.

Gheaus, Anca and Robeyns, Ingrid (2011) 'Equality promoting parental-leave', *Journal of Social Philosophy*, 42(2): 173–91.

Gilabert, Pablo (2011) 'Feasibility and socialism', *Journal of Political Philosophy*, 19: 52–63.

Glasgow, Joshua (2013) 'The shape of a life and the value of loss and gain', *Philosophical Studies*, 162(3), 665–82.

Goodin, Robert (1986) *Protecting the Vulnerable: A Reanalysis of our Social Responsibilities*, Chicago: University of Chicago Press.

Gutmann, Amy (1999) *Democratic Education*, Princeton, NJ: Princeton University Press.

Hannan, Sarah (2018) 'Why childhood is bad for children', *Journal of Applied Philosophy*, 35(1): 11–28.

Harris, George W. (1986) 'Fathers and fetuses', *Ethics*, 96 (3): 594–603.

Harris, Judith Rich (2006) *No Two Alike: Human Nature and Human Individuality*, New York: Norton & Co.

Hartas, Dimitra (2014) *Parenting, Family Policy and Children's Wellbeing in an Unequal Society*, Basingstoke: Palgrave.

Haslanger, Sally (2009) 'Family, ancestry and self: what is the moral significance of biological ties?', *Adoption & Culture*, 2(1): 91–122.

Heath, Joseph (1997) 'Intergenerational cooperation and distributive justice', *Canadian Journal of Philosophy*, 27(3): 361–76.

Hitchcock, David (2017) 'Critical thinking as an educational ideal', in David Hitchcock, *On Reasoning and Argument: Essays in Informal Logic and on Critical Thinking*, Dordrecht: Springer, pp 477–97.

Hobbes, Thomas (1839–1845) 'The elements of law', in *The English Works of Thomas Hobbes* (vols 1–11), ed William Molesworth, London, John Bohn, pp 77–229.

Hochschild, Arlie (1989) *The Second Shift: Working Parents and the Revolution at Home*, New York: Avon Books.

Hurka, Thomas (1993) *Perfectionism*, Oxford: Oxford University Press.

Jackson, Sonia and Martin, Pearl Y. (1998) 'Surviving the care system: education and resilience', *Journal of Adolescence*, 21(5): 569–583.

Jaggar, Alison M. (2009) 'L'imagination au pouvoir: comparing John Rawls's method of ideal theory with Iris Marion Young's method of critical theory', in Lisa Tessman (ed), *Feminist Ethics and Social and Political Philosophy: Theorizing the Non-Ideal*, Dordrecht: Springer, pp 59–66.

Kasser, Tim (2002) *The High Price of Materialism*, London: MIT Press.

Kelly, Erin and McPherson, Lionel (2001) 'On tolerating the unreasonable', *Journal of Political Philosophy*, 9(1): 38–55.

Klosko, George (1987) 'Presumptive benefit, fairness, and political obligation', *Philosophy and Public Affairs*, 16(3): 241–59.

Klosko, George (2004) *The Principle of Fairness and Political Obligation*, Lanham, MD: Rowman & Littlefield.

Kolers, Avery and Bayne, Tim (2001) '"Are you my mommy?" On the genetic basis of parenthood', *Journal of Applied Philosophy*, 18(3): 273–85.

Kymlicka, Will (1989) *Liberalism, Community and Culture*, Oxford: Oxford University Press.

Langer, Richard (1992) 'Abortion and the right to privacy', *Journal of Social Philosophy*, 23: 23–51.

Larmore, Charles (1987) *Patterns of Moral Complexity*, Cambridge: Cambridge University Press.

Lau, Matthew (2015) *The Right to be Loved*, Oxford: Oxford University Press.

Layard, Richard and Dunn, Judy (2009) *The Good Childhood: Searching for Values in a Competitive Age*, London: Penguin.

Lecce, Steven (2008) *Against Perfectionism: Defending Liberal Neutrality*, Toronto: University of Toronto Press.

Lloyd-Thomas, David (1988) *In Defence of Liberalism*, Oxford: Basil Blackwell.

Lomasky, Loren (1987) *Persons, Rights and the Moral Community*, Oxford: Oxford University Press.

Macedo, Stephen (2009) *Diversity and Distrust: Civic Education in a Multicultural Society*, Boston, MA: Harvard University Press.

Macleod, Colin M. (2010) 'Primary goods, capabilities and children', in Harry Brighouse and Ingrid Robeyns (eds) *Measuring Justice: Primary Goods and Capabilities*, Cambridge: Cambridge University Press, pp 174–292.

Macleod, Colin M. (2015) 'Parental competency and the right to parent', in Sarah Hannan, Samantha Brennan and Richard Vernon (eds) *Permissible Progeny*, Oxford: Oxford University Press, pp 227–42.

Magnusson, Erik (2018) 'Parental justice and the kids pay view', *Ethical Theory and Moral Practice*, published online, https://link.springer.com/article/10.1007/s10677-018-9937-z (accessed 26 October 2018).

Mason, Andrew (2011) 'Putting story-reading to bed: a reply to Segall', *Critical Review of International Social and Political Philosophy*, 14(1): 81–8.

Matthews, Gareth B. (2008) 'Getting beyond the deficit conception of childhood: thinking philosophically with children', in Michael Hand and Carrie Winstanley (eds) *Philosophy in Schools*, London: Continuum, pp 27–40.

Matthews, Gareth B. (2009) 'Philosophy and developmental psychology: outgrowing the deficit conception of childhood', in H. Siegel (ed.) *The Oxford Handbook of Philosophy of Education*, Oxford: Oxford University Press, pp 162–76.

McMahan, Jeff (2002) *The Ethics of Killing: Problems at the Margins of Life*, Oxford: Oxford University Press.

McPeck, John E. (1981) *Critical Thinking and Education*, New York: St Martin's Press.

Mills, Chris (2012) 'Can liberal perfectionism generate distinctive distributive principles?', *Philosophy and Public Issues*, 2(1): 123–52.

Millum, Joseph (2018) *The Moral Foundations of Parenthood*, Oxford: Oxford University Press.

Mookherjee, Monica (2008) 'Autonomy, force and cultural plurality', *Res Publica*, 14(3): 147–68.

Mookherjee, Monica (2011) *Women's Rights as Multicultural Claims: Reconfiguring Gender and Diversity in Political Philosophy*, Edinburgh: Edinburgh University Press.

Mullin, Amy (2014) 'Children, paternalism and the development of autonomy', *Ethical Theory and Moral Practice*, 17(3): 413–26.

Munoz-Plaza, Corrine, Quinn, Sandra and Rounds, Kathleen (2002) 'Lesbian, gay, bisexual and transgender students: perceived social support in the high school environment', *High School Journal*, 85: 52–63.

Nagel, Thomas (1970) *The Possibility of Altruism*, Chichester: Princeton University Press.

Nelson, Eric (2008) 'From primary goods to capabilities, distributive justice and the problem of neutrality', *Political Theory*, 36(1): 93–122.

Nelson, James L. (1991) 'Parental obligation and the ethics of surrogacy: a causal perspective', *Public Affairs Quarterly*, 5(1): 49–61.

Neufeld, Blain (2009) 'Coercion, the basic structure, and the family', *Journal of Social Philosophy*, 40: 37–54.

Neufeld, Blain and Van Schoelandt, Chad (2014) 'Political liberalism, ethos justice, and gender equality', *Law and Philosophy*, 33: 75–104.

Nozick, Robert (1974) *Anarchy, State and Utopia*, New York: Basic Books.

Nussbaum, Martha (2000) *Women and Human Development: The Capabilities Approach*, Cambridge: Cambridge University Press.

Okin, Susan Moller (1993) 'Is multiculturalism bad for women?', in Joshua Cohen, Matthew Howard and Martha Nussbaum (eds) *Is Multiculturalism Bad for Women? With Respondents*, Chichester: Princeton University Press, pp 7–26.

Okin, Susan Moller (1994) 'Political liberalism, justice, and gender', *Ethics*, 105(1): 23–43.

Olsaretti, Serena (2013) 'Children as public goods?', *Philosophy and Public Affairs*, 41(3): 226–58.

Olsaretti, Serena (2017) 'Children as negative externalities?', *Politics, Philosophy and Economics*, 16(2): 152–73.

O'Neill, Martin (2008) 'What should egalitarians believe?', *Philosophy and Public Affairs*, 36(2): 119–56.

O'Neill, Onora (1987) 'Abstraction, idealization and ideology in ethics', *Royal Institute of Philosophy Lecture Series*, 22, 55–69. doi:10.1017/S0957042X00003667

Parfit, Derek (1987) *Reasons and Persons*, Oxford: Clarendon Press.

Parfit, Derek (1997) 'Equality and priority', *Ratio*, 10(3): 202–21.

Parr, Tom (2018) 'How to identify disadvantage: taking the envy test seriously', *Political Studies*, 66(2): 306–22.

Peleg, N. (2013) 'Reconceptualising the child's right to development: children and the capability approach', *International Journal of Children's Rights*, 21(3): 523–42.

Peter, F. (2013) 'Epistemic foundations of political liberalism', *Journal of Moral Philosophy*, 10(5): 598–620.

Pickett, Kate and Wilkinson, Richard (2009a) *The Spirit Level: Why Equality is Better for Everyone*, London: Penguin.

Pickett, Kate and Wilkinson, Richard (2009b) *The Spirit Level: Why More Equal Societies Almost Always Do Better*, London: Allen Lane.

Piketty, Thomas (2014) *Capital in the 21st Century*, London: Belknap Press.

Pinker, Steven (2002) *The Blank Slate: The Modern Denial of Human Nature*, London: Penguin.

Pogge, Thomas (2010) 'A critique of the capability approach', in Harry Brighouse and Ingrid Robeyns (eds) *Measuring Justice: Primary Goods and Capabilities*, Cambridge: Cambridge University Press, pp 17–60.

Porter, Lindsey (2012) 'Adoption is not abortion-lite', *Journal of Applied Philosophy*, 29(1): 63–78.

Porter, Lindsey (2014) 'Why and how to prefer a causal account of parenthood', *Journal of Social Philosophy*, 45(2): 182–202.

Putman, Robert (2015) *Our Kids: The American Dream in Crisis*, New York: Simon & Schuster.

Quong, Jonathan (2004) 'The scope of public reason', *Political Studies*, 52(2): 233–50.

Quong, Jonathan (2011) *Liberalism without Perfection*, Oxford: Oxford University Press.

Rakowski, Eric (1993) *Equal Justice*, Oxford: Clarendon Press.

Rawls, John (1993) *Political Liberalism: Expanded Edition*, New York: Columbia University Press.

Rawls, John (1997) 'The idea of public reason revisited', *University of Chicago Law Review*, 64(3): 765–808.

Rawls, John (1999) *A Theory of Justice: Revised Edition*, Boston, MA: Harvard University Press.

Rawls, John (2001a) *Justice as Fairness: A Restatement*, London: Belknap Press.

Rawls, John (2001b) *The Law of Peoples: With 'the Idea of Public Reason Revisited'*, London: Belknap Press.

Raz, Joseph (1988) *The Morality of Freedom*, Oxford: Clarendon Press.

Richards, Norvin (2010) *The Ethics of Parenthood*, Oxford: Oxford University Press.

Richins, Marsha L. and Dawson, Scott (1992) 'A consumer values orientation for materialism and its measurement', *Journal of Consumer Research*, 23: 312–25.

Ripstein, Arthur (2009) *Force and Freedom: Kant's Legal and Political Philosophy*, Cambridge, MA: Harvard University Press.

Rotter, Julian B. (1954) *Social Learning and Clinical Psychology*, Englewood Cliffs, NJ: Prentice Hall.

Rotter, Julian B. (1990) 'Internal versus external control of reinforcement: a case history of a variable', *American Psychologist*, 45(4): 489–93.

Sadusky, Julia (2018) 'Loneliness and the celibate, gay Christian', ProQuest Dissertations, https://www.cpc.unc.edu/projects/addhealth/publications/8066 (accessed 22 October 2018).

Satz, Debra (2007) 'Equality, adequacy and education for citizenship', *Ethics*, 117(4): 623–48.

Savin-Williams, Ritch and Ream, Geoffrey (2003) 'Sex variations in the disclosure to parents of same-sex attractions', *Journal of Family Psychology*, 17: 429–38.

Savin-Williams, Ritch C. and Vrangalova, Zhana (2013) 'Mostly heterosexual as a distinct sexual orientation group: a systematic review of the empirical evidence', *Developmental Review*, 33(1): 58–88.

Scanlon, Thomas (2003) 'The diversity of objections to inequality', in Thomas Scanlon, *The Difficulty of Tolerance: Essays in Political Philosophy*, Cambridge: Cambridge University Press, pp 202–18.

Scheffler, Samuel (2013) *Death and the Afterlife*, ed Niko Kolodny, Oxford: Oxford University Press.

Schemmel, Christian (2011) 'Why relational egalitarians should care about distributions', *Social Theory and Practice*, 37(3): 365–90.

Schmuck, Peter, Kasser, Tim and Ryan, Richard M. (2000) 'Intrinsic and extrinsic goals: their structure and relationship to wellbeing in German and U.S. college students', *Social Indicators Research*, 50: 225–41.

Schor, Juliet, (2004) *Born to Buy: The Commercialized Child and the New Consumer Culture*, London: Scribner.

Schouten, Gina (2017) 'Citizenship, reciprocity and the gendered division of labour', *Politics, Philosophy and Economics*, 15(2): 174–209.

Schouten, Gina (2018) 'Political liberalism and autonomy education: are citizenship based arguments enough?' *Philosophical Studies*, 175(5): 1071–93.

Schwartz, Barry (1994) *The Costs of Living: How Market Freedom Erodes the Best Things in Life*, New York: Norton.

Schweiger, Gottfried, Graf, Gunter and Cabezas, Mar (2016) 'Justice and disadvantages during childhood: what does the capability approach have to offer?', *Ethical Perspectives*, 23(1): 73–99.

Segall, Shlomi (2013) *Equality and Opportunity*, Oxford: Oxford University Press.

Sen, Amartya (1987) 'Equality of what?', in Sterling M. McMurrin (ed.) *Liberty, Equality and Law: Selected Tanner Lectures on Moral Philosophy*, Salt Lake City: University of Utah Press, pp 137–62.

Sen, Amartya (1999) *Development as Freedom*, Oxford: Oxford University Press.

Sen, Amartya (2000) *Development as Freedom*, New York: Anchor Books.

Shapiro, Tamar (1999) 'What is a child?', *Ethics*, 109(4): 715–38.

Sheets, Raymond L., Jr. and Mohr, Jonathan J. (2009) 'Perceived social support from friends and family and psychosocial functioning in bisexual young adult college students', *Journal of Counseling Psychology*, 56(1): 152–63.

Shields, Liam (2012) 'The prospects for sufficientarianism', *Utilitas*, 24(1): 101–17.

Shields, Liam (2013) 'From Rawlsian autonomy to sufficient opportunity in education', *Politics, Philosophy and Economics*, 14(1): 53–66.

Shields, Liam (2016) 'How bad can a good enough parent be?', *Canadian Journal of Philosophy*, 46(2): 163–82.

Shiffrin, Seana Valentine (1999) 'Wrongful life, procreative responsibility and the significance of harm', *Legal Theory* 5: 117–48.

Singer, Peter (1972) 'Famine, affluence and morality', *Philosophy and Public Affairs*, 1(3): 229–23.

Sinnott-Armstrong, Walter (2006) *Moral Skepticisms*, New York: Oxford University Press.

Slote, Michael (1983) *Goods and Virtues*, Oxford: Clarendon Press.

Stemplowska, Zosia (2008) 'What's ideal about ideal theory', *Social Theory and Practice*, 34(3): 319–40.

Stevenson, Betsey and Wolfers, Justin (2008) 'Economic growth and subjective well-being: re-assessing the Easterlin paradox', *Brookings Panel on Economic Activity*, April.

Strawson, Peter (2008) 'Freedom and resentment', in Peter Strawson, *Freedom and Resentment and Other Essays*, London: Routledge.

Swift, Adam (2003) *How Not to be a Hypocrite: School Choice for a Morally Perplexed Parent*, London: Routledge.

Taylor, Robert (2004) 'Self-realisation and the priority of equality of opportunity', *Journal of Moral Philosophy*, 1(3): 333–47.

Temkin, Larry (2000) 'Equality, priority and the levelling down objection', in Matthew Clayton and Andrew Williams (eds) *The Ideal of Equality*, London: Macmillan, pp 126–61.

Terlazzo, Rosa (2015) 'Conceptualising adaptive preferences respectfully: an indirectly substantive account', *Journal of Political Philosophy*, 24(2): 206–26.

Thomson, Judith Jarvis (1971) 'A defence of abortion', *Philosophy and Public Affairs*, 1(1): 47–66.

Tomasi, John (2012) *Free Market Fairness*, Oxford: Princeton University Press.

Tomlin, Patrick (2013) 'Should kids pay their own way?', *Political Studies*, 63: 663–78.

Tomlin, Patrick (2016) 'Saplings or caterpillars? Trying to understand children's wellbeing', *Journal of Applied Philosophy*, 35: 29–46.

Vallentyne, Peter (2013) 'Rights and duties of childrearing', *William and Mary Bill of Rights Journal*, 11: 991–1010.

Vallier, Kevin (2014) *Liberal Politics and Public Faith: Beyond Separation*, London: Routledge.

Vallier, Kevin (2017) 'On Jonathan Quong's sectarian political liberalism', *Criminal Law and Philosophy*, 11(1): 175–94.

Van Bergen, Diana D., Bos, Henry M. W., van Lisdonk, Jantine, Keuzenkamp, Saskia, and Sandfort, Theo G. M. (2013) 'Victimization and suicidality amongst Dutch lesbian, gay and bisexual youths', *American Journal of Public Health*, 103(1): 70–2.

Velleman, J. David (2005) 'Family history', *Philosophical Papers*, 34(3): 357–78.

Waldron, Jeremy (1989) 'Autonomy and perfectionism in Raz's *Morality of Freedom*', *Southern California Law Review*, 62: 1138–52.

Waldron, Jeremy (1999) *Law and Disagreement*, Oxford: Oxford University Press.

Walker, Melanie (2006) *Higher Education Pedagogies: A Capabilities Approach*, London: Open University Press.

Wall, Steven (1998) *Liberalism, Perfectionism and Restraint*, Cambridge: Cambridge University Press.

Wall, Steven (2010) 'Neutralism for perfectionists: the case of restricted state neutrality', *Ethics*, 120(2): 232–56.

Wallace-Wells, David (2019) *The Uninhabitable Earth*, London: Penguin.

Ward, Colleen and Kennedy, Antony (1992) 'Locus of control, mood disturbance, and social difficulty during cross-cultural transitions', *International Journal of Intercultural Relations*, 16(2): 175–94.

Wijedasa, Dinithi (2017) '"People like me don't have much of a chance in life": comparing the locus of control of young people in foster care with that of adoptees, children from disadvantaged backgrounds and children in the general population', *Adoption and Fostering*, 41(1): 5–19.

Williams, Andrew (1998) 'Incentives, inequality and publicity', *Philosophy and Public Affairs*, 27(3): 225–47.

Williams, Bernard (1962) 'The idea of equality', in Peter Laslett and Walter G. Runciman (eds) *Philosophy, Politics, and Society* (series II), London: Basil Blackwell, pp 110–31.

Williams, Bernard (1981) *Moral Luck*, Cambridge: Cambridge University Press.

Index